The Albert Einstein Story

Jake Ronaldson

Level 1
(1000-word)

IBC パブリッシング

はじめに

　ラダーシリーズは、「はしご (ladder)」を使って一歩一歩上を目指すように、学習者の実力に合わせ、無理なくステップアップできるよう開発された英文リーダーのシリーズです。

　リーディング力をつけるためには、繰り返したくさん読むこと、いわゆる「多読」がもっとも効果的な学習法であると言われています。多読では、「1. 速く 2. 訳さず英語のまま 3. なるべく辞書を使わず」に読むことが大切です。スピードを計るなど、速く読むよう心がけましょう（たとえば TOEIC[R] テストの音声スピードはおよそ1分間に150語です）。そして1語ずつ訳すのではなく、英語を英語のまま理解するくせをつけるようにします。こうして読み続けるうちに語感がついてきて、だんだんと英語が理解できるようになるのです。まずは、ラダーシリーズの中からあなたのレベルに合った本を選び、少しずつ英文に慣れ親しんでください。たくさんの本を手にとるうちに、英文書がすらすら読めるようになってくるはずです。

《本シリーズの特徴》
- 中学校レベルから中級者レベルまで5段階に分かれています。自分に合ったレベルからスタートしてください。
- クラシックから現代文学、ノンフィクション、ビジネスと幅広いジャンルを扱っています。あなたの興味に合わせてタイトルを選べます。
- 巻末のワードリストで、いつでもどこでも単語の意味を確認できます。レベル1、2では、文中の全ての単語が、レベル3以上は中学校レベル外の単語が掲載されています。
- カバーにヘッドホーンマークのついているタイトルは、オーディオ・サポートがあります。ウェブから購入／ダウンロードし、リスニング教材としても併用できます。

《使用語彙について》
レベル1：中学校で学習する単語約1000語
レベル2：レベル1の単語＋使用頻度の高い単語約300語
レベル3：レベル1の単語＋使用頻度の高い単語約600語
レベル4：レベル1の単語＋使用頻度の高い単語約1000語
レベル5：語彙制限なし

Contents

Young Einstein 3

Einstein's School Years 6

Important Books 9

Switzerland 12

Difficult Times 17

Einstein's Miracle Year 21

Einstein and Planck 26

General Relativity 31

Proving Einstein's Theory 41

To Berlin 46

World War I 51

Einstein and Eddington 59

The Greatest Scientist in the World 66

To America 72

Einstein's Last Days 81

Word List 86

【読み始める前に】

本文中に出てくるキーワードです。はじめに目を通しておくとよいでしょう。さらに詳しく知りたい方は巻末の辞書を参照してください。

- ☐ math 数学
- ☐ Euclid ユークリッド原論
- ☐ magnetic fields 磁場、磁界
- ☐ theory of relativity 相対性理論
- ☐ mechanical forces 機械力
- ☐ speed of light 光の速度
- ☐ telescope 望遠鏡
- ☐ properties of waves 波動の性質
- ☐ gravity 重力
- ☐ magnet 磁石
- ☐ physics 物理学
- ☐ microscope 顕微鏡
- ☐ beam of light 光線
- ☐ particle 粒子
- ☐ photon 光量子
- ☐ quantum physics 量子物理学
- ☐ atom 原子
- ☐ dust particles 塵状の個体粒子
- ☐ liquid 液体
- ☐ energy and matter エネルギーと質量
- ☐ mass 質量
- ☐ nuclear explosion 原子核の爆発
- ☐ space-time 時空
- ☐ equation 方程式
- ☐ special relativity 特殊相対性理論
- ☐ general theory of relativity 一般相対性理論
- ☐ black hole ブラックホール
- ☐ molecules 微粒子
- ☐ eclipse 日食
- ☐ orbit 軌道
- ☐ cosmology 宇宙論
- ☐ quantum theory 量子論
- ☐ unified field theory 統一場理論
- ☐ atom bomb 原子爆弾

登場人物紹介

Hermann　ヘルマン　アインシュタインの父
Pauline　パウリーネ　アインシュタインの母
Jakob　ヤコブ　アインシュタインの叔父
Marie Winteler　マリー・ヴィンテラー　最初のガールフレンド
Mileva Maric　ミレーバ・マリッチ　最初の妻
Hans Albert　ハンス・アルベルト　アインシュタインの長男
Eduard　エドゥアルト　アインシュタインの次男
Elsa　エルザ　2番目の妻

アルベルト・アインシュタインの生涯

1879年3月14日　ドイツの小都市ウルムのユダヤ人家庭の長男として生まれる

1880年（1歳）　父（ヘルマン）の事業が失敗し、ミュンヘンに移る

1885年（6歳）　母（パウリーネ）の影響でバイオリンを始める。モーツァルトをよく弾いた。国民学校に入学

1888年（9歳）　ルイトポルト・ギムナジウムに入学。10歳になると、ユークリッド原論を読んだ

1894年（15歳）　父の会社が倒産し、家族はミラノ近郊の町に移住。アインシュタインはミュンヘンに残るが、その後教師との諍いもあり退学する

1896年（17歳）　スイスのチューリッヒにあるスイス連邦工科大学に入学。その後、結婚相手となるミレーバ・マリッチと出会う

1900年（21歳）　卒業したが、科学者としての就職先がいっさい見つからず、家庭教師や代理教員として働く

1902年（23歳）　スイスのベルンに移り、特許局での仕事に就く

1903年（24歳）　ミレーバと結婚、翌年長男のハンスが生まれる

1905年（26歳）　「ブラウン運動の理論」、「特殊相対性理論」などの論文を発表、アインシュタインにとって「奇跡の年」となる

1907年（28歳）　$E=mc^2$の式を発表

1909年（30歳）　チューリッヒ大学の助教授となる、翌年には次男のエドゥアルト誕生

1911年（32歳）　「空はなぜ青いのか」という質問の答えを見いだす

1913年（34歳）　ベルリンに移住することになるが、妻は子供を連れチューリッヒに戻り、別居状態となる

1916年（37歳）　「一般相対性理論」を発表

1919年（40歳）　ミレーバと離婚し、その後エルザと再婚する

1921年～22年（42歳～43歳）　アメリカ、イギリス、フランス、日本、パレスティナなどを訪問、ノーベル賞受賞

1932年（53歳）　ナチ政権下のドイツからアメリカへ。翌年にはプリンストンの研究所の教授となる

1939年（60歳）　ルーズベルト大統領宛に原爆についての書簡を送る

1948年（69歳）　イスラエル建国に際し、大統領就任を要請されるが断る

1955年（76歳）　4月18日、76歳の生涯を終える

The Albert Einstein Story

Young Einstein

Albert Einstein was born on March 14, 1879 in the city of Ulm, Germany. His parents' names were Hermann and Pauline.

Einstein's father Hermann was friendly, kind, and intelligent. He was also very good at math when he was young.

Einstein's mother Pauline was the boss in the family. She came from a rich family, and she was very intelligent. She loved music and was a very good piano player.

When Einstein was born, his family sold beds, but the company closed down. They soon moved to the big city of Munich. In Munich, Hermann opened a new company with his brother Jakob.

Einstein was not like other children. When he was a baby, he did not say his first words until after he was two years old. Hermann and Pauline were very worried about him, and they took him to see many doctors, but no one knew what the problem was. People around him worried that he might never learn to speak well!

Until he was 10 years old, Einstein was not very good at talking. Even when he became an adult, he said, "I rarely think in words at all."

Einstein was very different from other boys. When he was young, he did not like to play sports and games with the other children. He liked to go and sit by himself and think and dream.

Einstein really liked blocks, and he also liked to build houses from playing cards. They say that he could make a house that was 14 stories tall! He did not worry about how many times the houses fell down, and he worked on them for hours and hours.

Einstein also loved music and started to play the violin when he was very young. He loved Mozart, and he practiced playing his music for hours and hours.

Einstein was better at science than music, but they say that if he ever found a question he could not answer, he went and listened to music. Music always helped him find the answer he was looking for.

Einstein's School Years

Today, many people believe that Einstein was not a good student, and there is a famous story that he once failed math. It is a great story because it gives hope to many poor math students, but it is not true.

The truth is that Einstein was one of the best students in the school. He loved math so much that he often studied difficult math books by himself during the summer. He read Euclid when he was just 10 years old.

Einstein was intelligent, but he did not like to be told what to do. He sometimes made his teachers very angry. He was once made to leave school, and some of his teachers said that he was lazy. One of them said he would never do anything special in his life!

Einstein liked to spend a lot of time alone, and it was very easy to make him angry. He often used to throw things at the other children, and one time he threw a chair at his violin teacher!

When Einstein was nine, he started going to a school that was well known for teaching math and science.

Einstein was not interested in space and time until he got older. Most children think about space and time when they are very young, but Einstein did not start thinking about them until he was an adult. Because he was an adult, Einstein was able to think about them more deeply.

Einstein once said that he believed that being a slow child was what helped him to explain the theory of relativity.

Einstein's favorite toy was a compass. One day, when he was sick in bed, his father gave it to him to make him feel better. Einstein loved seeing the way the needle always moved to point north. It made him very interested in the way nature worked.

Young Einstein learned that the compass moved because of magnetic fields, and in his future work, fields were always at the center of his science.

This was the first time that Einstein had the idea that there was more to the world than just the things you could see and touch. He got the idea that he wanted to learn about more than just the mechanical forces in the world. He wanted to understand the hidden ones too.

Important Books

During Einstein's school days, he was given a set of books called *People's Books on Natural Science* by Aaron Bernstein. Einstein loved the books, and they were very important in helping to make Einstein a great scientist.

The first book talked about the speed of light, and it had a strong effect on Einstein's thinking. First, Bernstein asked the reader to imagine he or she was on a fast-moving train. What happens if you shoot a bullet through the window on one side and it goes out the window on the other side? If you are inside the train, it might seem that the bullet moved at an angle. Why? Because of the time it took to move through the train. The bullet goes straight, but the train is moving.

Now, let's imagine that the Earth is a train. Bernstein said that the same must be true for light in a telescope. This is because the earth is moving through space very fast.

Now, imagine that someone shoots two bullets. One is shot from close to the train and one is shot from far away. The first bullet will be moving faster, so the angle will be smaller and the second bullet will be moving slower, so the angle will be bigger. But with light, there is no change. Whether a star is close or far away, the angle is always the same.

This means that light always moves at the same speed. It is the most general law in nature. This was very important for Einstein later!

Bernstein said that all the forces in nature could be tied together. He said that since light had the properties of a wave, gravity might also be one. He said that there are laws that are hidden behind everything in nature, and it is possible for people to find them. When Einstein read this, he knew that he wanted to be a scientist and help find them.

Switzerland

In 1894, when Einstein was 15, his father's company went bankrupt. His parents and sister moved to Italy. They lived in Milan and then moved to a small town close to it. The new town was called Pavia.

Einstein stayed in Munich. He wanted to finish school, but he had a problem with one of the teachers.

The teacher thought that Einstein did not give him enough respect. Einstein was always sitting in the very back, smiling and not listening to what the teacher said. One day, the teacher got angry and said that Einstein had to respect him.

Soon after, Einstein quit the school. We do not know if Einstein was made to leave the school or not, but it is often said that he wanted to leave.

One day, Einstein arrived in Italy and told his parents that he never wanted to go back to Germany! He said that he was going to study by himself and try to enter a new school in Zurich. He lived with his parents in the spring and summer of 1895.

Einstein also helped his parents with the family's electric company. He learned many things about magnets and electricity at this time. Everyone in the family said that he was a great worker.

One day, his uncle and an engineer asked him to help them with some calculations. They had been trying to find the answer for days and days, but Einstein was able to do it in just 15 minutes!

Pavia was in the mountains, and during this time, Einstein also spent many happy hours walking in the mountains.

In the fall of that year, Einstein went to Zurich and tried to enter a school called the Eidgenössische Technische Hochschule. He did well in math and physics, but he was not able to enter the school because he was not good enough in other areas of the test.

Einstein did not want to give up, so he moved to the town of Aarau near Zurich. He spent another year studying there. The school in Aarau was very good for Einstein because the teachers wanted the students to be creative and free. Einstein was able to study when he wanted and how he wanted.

In Aarau, Einstein also enjoyed walking, playing the violin, and spending time with his first girlfriend, Marie Winteler.

In 1896, Einstein took the test at the Eidgenössische Technische Hochschule again. This time, he passed. He studied to become a teacher of physics and math.

Einstein did not like listening to the teachers, so he did not go to class very often. He was not a bad student, but not a good one either.

If not for his friend Marcel Grossmann, Einstein might have had to leave this school too. While Einstein worked in the library, Grossmann took excellent notes at the lectures, and Einstein used them to study from.

When Einstein was at the Polytechnic in Zurich, he was very popular with women. He often worked as a musician, and ladies' clubs sometimes invited him to play his violin at their parties.

Einstein had many chances to meet women at these parties. He was very good looking, and his violin playing was beautiful. At one of these parties, he met a woman named Mileva Maric.

Like Einstein, Mileva was a very special person. In those days, women almost never studied math and physics at a high level. She was one of the only women in the school.

Einstein fell in love with her. She was someone that he could talk about his ideas to, and she often checked the math in his papers!

Difficult Times

After he finished his studies in 1901, Einstein found that he could not get a job anywhere. At one time, he even thought about giving up his dream of being a scientist. He almost took a job selling insurance!

Einstein felt that he could not do anything well. Things got so bad that he even wrote a letter to his family saying that it would have been better if he had never been born.

After finishing school, Einstein did many different jobs. He worked as a teacher and tutor, but he could not find a job as a scientist.

Einstein's father wanted to help him,

and he wrote letters to some people that he knew. He asked one friend if he could use Einstein as a research assistant, but the friend said that he did not know of any jobs.

It is sad to say, but when Einstein's father died, he believed that his son would never be successful in life.

In 1902, Einstein moved to Bern, Switzerland. He could not get a job as a scientist, but his friend from school, Marcel Grossmann, helped him to find a job as a patent clerk. At this time, he also got married to Mileva.

Both Einstein's family and Mileva's told them that they should not get married, but they did not listen. They were in love, and they wanted to be together.

The Einsteins had their first child,

Einstein with his wife, Mileva

Hans Albert, in 1904. Their second child, Eduard, was born in 1910. They did not have much money at all, and all of them had to live in just two rooms.

Einstein worked six days a week at his job. It was not an exciting job, but it was easy for him, and he had a lot of time to think. And what did he think about? The universe, of course.

Albert Einstein was a dreamer. He was not a scientist who worked in a lab doing experiments every day. He had no telescope or microscope. He was a man who liked to sit and think.

Einstein's great ideas did not just come from his intelligence or hard work. They came from his imagination and his creativity. In his free time, he thought about things like what it would be like to ride beside a beam of light.

Times were difficult, but soon Einstein was going to do some of his greatest work.

Einstein's Miracle Year

Einstein lived at a time when many great men were changing the way people thought. Pablo Picasso, James Joyce, Sigmund Freud, and many more were bringing strange new ideas to the world. But Einstein changed the world more than any of them.

1905 has been called Einstein's "miracle year." In his free time, he put out four important papers. In the first one, he answered the question "What is light?" It showed that light comes as a particle called a photon. Today, we use that idea in television and lasers, and it was the very beginning of quantum physics!

In his next paper, Einstein wrote about something that everyone understands today. He wrote about atoms. But at the time he wrote his paper, people did not believe in them. He proved that they can make small dust particles move in liquid. He was even able to calculate the size of atoms.

Those two papers would have been a great success for most scientists. But Einstein had just begun.

Einstein's third paper is the one he is best remembered for today. It was here that he told the world that $E=mc^2$.

$E=mc^2$ sounds very difficult, but it is actually easy to understand. It means that energy and matter are the same thing.

Because matter and energy are the

same thing, energy can become matter and matter can become energy. Even a tiny piece of matter can have a very, very big amount of energy in it.

Einstein's third paper helped us to understand the stars in the sky. Before Einstein, no one knew where the light of the stars came from. He told us that energy (E) is the same as mass (M) times the speed of light (C) squared. He told us that even something as small as an atom can have a lot of energy in it. Thanks to Einstein, we now know that the light of the stars comes from the energy coming out of atoms in nuclear explosions.

Einstein's third paper and E=mc^2 is the most famous, but the next one was even more important. It was his special theory of relativity.

From the time he was 16, Einstein often enjoyed thinking about what it might be like to ride a beam of light. In those days, it was just a dream, but he returned to it, and it changed his life.

One day in the spring of 1905, Einstein was riding a bus, and he looked back at a big clock behind him. He imagined what would happen if his bus were going as fast as the speed of light.

When Einstein began to move at the speed of light, the hands of the clock stopped moving! This was one of the most important moments of Einstein's life!

When Einstein looked back at the real clock, time was moving normally, but on the bus moving at the speed of light, time was not moving at all. Why? Because at the speed of light, he is moving so fast that the light from the clock cannot catch up to him. The faster something moves in space, the slower it moves in time.

This was the beginning of Einstein's special theory of relativity. It says that space and time are the same thing. You cannot have space without time, and you cannot have time without space. He called it "space-time."

No scientist has ever done anything like what Einstein did in that one year. He was very ambitious. Einstein once said, "I want to know God's thoughts…"

Einstein wanted an equation that was very short, but which explained all of the laws of physics! He wanted to put the beauty and the power of the universe into just one equation that would explain everything. That was his big dream in life.

For Einstein, math was the language of nature. The really great thing that Einstein was able to do was to see math equations in nature and the world.

Einstein and Planck

Einstein sent his papers to some of the most famous science journals in Europe. But what would you do if you got a paper from Einstein? He was not a scientist and no one had heard of him before. Would you put the paper in your journal?

Even more important, his ideas sounded crazy. They went against everything that all of the scientists in the world believed in those days.

Everyone said no to Einstein at first. No one in the world of science was interested in what he was saying.

Einstein tried again and again to get his papers into journals, but he had no luck at all. As time went on, he began to worry that no one would ever believe him. He became very sad.

After about five months with no luck, a man named Max Planck read Einstein's papers. He was the greatest physicist in Europe. He was one of just a few people who could understand what Einstein was saying.

When Planck read Einstein's papers, he knew that his ideas were important. In June 1905, Einstein's paper on relativity was published in the *Annalen Der Physik*. It was the most famous physics journal in Europe!

After reading Einstein's paper, Max Planck wanted to know more about him. At the time Einstein's paper went into the *Annalen Der Physik*, he was still trying to find a job as a scientist or teacher. Planck knew that Einstein was not famous, but he did not know that Einstein was just a patent clerk.

Later, when the two men met, Einstein said, "Within a few hours we were true friends, as though our dreams…were made for each other."

In 1907, Einstein was asked to write a new paper to explain special relativity. He went back to start thinking about relativity again. But he saw that there was a problem. His theory was too limited.

Einstein's theory was called "special relativity." This is because it was only about things that always moved at the same speed. It could only be used in special situations. Special relativity was only for things that moved in one direction and whose speed never changed.

For Einstein, special relativity was not enough. He wanted to understand the real world. He wanted to know what things were like in the universe, in the sky, and in the stars that we see every night. When things accelerate, you cannot use the theory of special relativity. This is a big problem because in our universe, everything accelerates.

Einstein knew that he had to find a theory that was not just for "special" cases. He needed a "general theory of relativity." The most difficult part of making this general theory was to explain gravity.

Because of Newton, we know that everything in the universe is held together by gravity, but no one knew how gravity worked. Einstein now began to work on a new theory to explain both gravity and time.

General Relativity

His papers were now famous, but at the age of 29, Einstein was still working at his old job. It was two years since he put out his paper on special relativity. Einstein knew that it was now time to work on a paper with a general theory of relativity.

Isaac Newton was the most important man in the history of science before Einstein. Almost everything that people believed about physics came from Newton's theories. Now, almost 250 years after Newton sat under his apple tree and saw the apple fall, Einstein was going to change the way that everyone thought about gravity.

When Newton saw the apple fall, he thought that it was because the earth was pulling it down. The problem with that idea is that in physics, things are never 'pulled.' They are always 'pushed.'

Newton knew that there was some problem with his theory, but in those days, it was not possible to answer the question. He had to stop working on it because he could not find the answer.

In his new theory, Einstein was trying to answer the question that Newton

The first manuscript of Einstein's Theory of Relativity

could not: What was making the apple fall to the earth? What was 'pushing' it?

Everyone told Einstein that the question was too difficult. Even Max Planck, the man who had read Einstein's papers and believed in him, told him that he should try to answer some other question.

Planck said to Einstein, "Even if you find the answer, no one will believe you!"

Einstein had no idea where to begin. No one else in the world was trying to answer this question.

Einstein had no one to help him, and there were no books that he could look for ideas in. But Einstein knew a way to answer the question.

Einstein went back to his favorite

technique, the thought experiment. One day while he was at work, he looked out the window. He saw a man across the street working on a roof.

Einstein asked himself, "What will happen if the man falls off the roof?" When most of us think about this question, we only think about the very end when the man hits the ground. But Einstein thought about what happened before that. He thought about the man as he was falling.

Einstein had the idea that while the man was falling, he would not feel his own weight. He would be weightless.

Here is an easy way to understand it. If a man is in a very, very, very tall elevator and the elevator falls, what will happen?

The man can float around in the elevator, and he will not feel that anything is strange. People outside can see that he is falling, but he does not know it. If he looks out, it might look as if people around him are going up!

The falling man has no weight, but what does that mean? Think about it. It means that when the man is falling because of gravity, it is the same as if he is just floating in space where there is no gravity.

If you can say that the man is moving toward the earth, you can also say that the earth is moving toward him!

Another way to think of it is like a train. Imagine you are on a train and it stops at a station. If another train starts to move while yours is stopped, it can look as if your train is moving when it is not.

Einstein used equations to show that gravity was caused by the mixing of matter, motion, and energy. Einstein knew from special relativity that acceleration can change the way time is measured, and he knew that gravity is the same as acceleration. That means that gravity could also affect the measurements of time and space!

Gravity can make time move more slowly and it can warp space. It sounds strange, but it is true. If there is an object in space, its mass warps the space and time around it.

Here is a very easy way to understand it. Imagine there is a piece of cloth that is stretched out, and you put a heavy ball on it. The ball will warp the cloth, and if you put another smaller ball on the cloth, it will move closer to the big ball. This is because the fabric is stretched, not because the big ball is pulling the small ball.

We can use this idea to understand gravity and why the earth goes around the sun. The mass of the sun warps the space around it. Because of this, space behind the earth pushes the earth toward the sun.

Another interesting idea is that a clock moves more slowly when it comes close to the sun. This is because mass can affect time the same way it affects space.

One of the strangest ideas that comes from his theory is the black hole. If a big thing like a star becomes very, very small when it has no more fuel, its gravity might get so strong that it takes in all the light and matter that comes close to it. Time becomes so slow that it almost stops, and no light can leave it. At the time, Einstein did not think that black holes were real, but scientists have shown that he was right!

While he was working on his new theory of general relativity, Einstein was finally able to quit his old job. He was able to get a teaching job at the University of Zurich. Now he could work on science full time.

It was a little late because he was 32 years old, but Einstein was finally able to leave Bern and do what he always wanted to.

It was also in 1911 that Einstein answered one of the oldest and most famous questions of all time: Why is the sky blue? Every young boy and girl in the world wants to know the answer. Thanks to Einstein, we can tell them.

The reason is that light from the sun hits molecules in the sky. As you know, red, blue, green, yellow, and all the other colors are in light. But blue is scattered the most when it hits a molecule. Before Einstein, no one knew if the scattering was because of dust or molecules. Einstein's calculations showed that it was from molecules. Now we know we can answer our children's question.

This was also the year that more and more people started reading the four papers that Einstein wrote in 1905. He began to have chances to meet with some of the greatest scientists in Europe. Einstein was asked to speak all over Europe, and soon everyone became very excited about his ideas. Some people believed him, and some people did not. Relativity was just a theory, and if it could not be tested, there was no way to make everyone believe that he was right.

Proving Einstein's Theory

Einstein needed to think of an experiment to show his theory was right. This time, it had to be a real one, not a thought experiment.

One day in 1911, he had an idea. His idea was to shine a beam of light through an area where space was curved. Einstein said that light always moves straight, but space is curved. If it looked like the light was not straight, that would show that it was space that was curved.

Where could Einstein find something that was so big it could curve light? There was nothing on Earth that could do it. His idea was to use the sun.

Einstein knew that if light that came from a far away star came close to the sun, the light should look like it was curving.

Einstein's next problem was that the sun was too bright. How can you see light beside something like the sun? Then Einstein remembered the eclipse. Einstein's idea was that when there was an eclipse, he could see the light from the stars behind the sun curving.

In 1912, Einstein was ready to try his great experiment. He wrote a new paper and asked astronomers to try his experiment for him.

Einstein was very excited, and he waited for someone to do the experiment. But no one tried it.

Einstein wrote to famous astronomers

and asked them to help him, but no one did. Many of the astronomers were too busy to do his experiment, and some did not believe him. He had to wait.

Finally, a man at the Berlin Observatory named Erwin Finlay-Freundlich said that he wanted to help Einstein.

Freundlich was a young man. He was not even 30 years old, and he wanted to be a part of something big and important. He was about to get married, and Einstein asked him to come to Zurich for his honeymoon. Freundlich's new wife was probably not too happy, but he came to see Einstein.

When Freundlich and his wife got off the train, Einstein was waiting for them. He took them to where he was giving a big speech. In the middle of the speech,

Einstein suddenly pointed to Freundlich. He said that Freundlich was going to help him prove his theory of general relativity.

After the speech, Einstein and Freundlich talked more about general relativity and their great experiment. It was probably not too much fun for Freundlich's new wife, but it was a great moment for science!

Einstein and Freundlich knew that the next eclipse was going to be in the Crimea in Russia on August 21, 1914.

Freundlich told his boss that he wanted to help Einstein, but Freundlich's boss became very angry. He thought that Freundlich was crazy to be working with Einstein. He told Freundlich not to do it.

Freundlich wrote to an American astronomer named William Wallace Campbell to ask him to come to take photos of the eclipse.

Campbell said that he would come to Russia to help Einstein and Freundlich. It was a very exciting moment for the three men. If their experiment was successful, it would prove that Einstein's theory was right and change physics forever.

To Berlin

While Einstein was waiting for the great experiment, Max Planck asked him if he would like to come to Berlin.

Planck wanted to bring Einstein to Berlin because he had become so famous. The Kaiser had asked Planck to find the best scientists in Germany, and Einstein was one of the first people that Planck thought of. If he could bring Einstein to Berlin, people would say that the city was the center of science in Europe.

On July 11, 1913, Planck and another famous German scientist named Walter Nernst came to Zurich to see Einstein. They came to talk to Einstein face to face and ask him to come back to Germany with them.

Planck and Nernst told Einstein that this was a great chance for him. He had a chance to be a professor and a member of the famous Prussian Academy. He did not have to teach, and he could have as much help as he needed in his research.

Einstein felt very good. He remembered the long years when he dreamed of becoming a professor and working at a famous university. But Einstein did not say yes immediately.

Einstein told Planck that he had to think about it. Einstein told him that he was going to take a walk for a few hours. He promised to come to meet them at the station before they left.

Einstein said that he was going to

get some flowers on his walk. He said, "If the flowers are red, I am coming to Germany and if the flowers are white, I will not."

Some people say that Einstein did this because he remembered all the times he had been rejected in the past. Einstein wanted to be wanted.

Einstein took a long walk. He had lived in Zurich for many years, and he loved the city. His wife wanted to stay in Zurich too. But working in Berlin was a dream come true.

Planck and Nernst waited for Einstein at the station. They were very nervous. Would he come to Germany with them? Then they saw Einstein. He had some red flowers in his hand. He said, "Gentlemen, I will go to Germany. I'm going to become one of you."

Einstein went to Germany in April, 1914. It was time to start his new job at the Kaiser Wilhelm Institute. The scientists there were some of the best in Europe.

Einstein's research was going very well, but his family life was not. Mileva did not like Berlin, and they began to fight.

Einstein liked being with a cousin of his named Elsa, and he often talked about how much he liked her. At these times, Mileva got very angry, and the two would have big fights.

Things became so bad that one day Einstein gave Mileva a list. It was all the things that she had to do if she wanted to stay married to him! Einstein said she had to bring his food to him in his room and speak to him only when he wanted to talk. But Mileva said no. She moved out of the house and told Einstein that she did not love him.

Einstein did not want to be married either, but he did not have enough money to give to Mileva. He told her that someday he was going to win the Nobel Prize. If she gave him a divorce, when he won the Nobel, he would give her the prize money. She thought about it for a week and said yes.

When Mileva left Berlin, Einstein took her and the children to the train station to say goodbye. He started to cry.

World War I

For Einstein to win the Nobel Prize, the eclipse experiment had to go well. Freundlich and Campbell went to the Crimea for the great experiment. The Crimea was a dangerous place, and even worse, World War I was about to start.

On August 1, Germany declared war against Russia. Freundlich and Campbell were already in the Crimea, and Einstein had no way to tell them that they were in danger.

One day, some Russian soldiers saw Freundlich with his telescope. Campbell was American, so they were not worried about him, but Freundlich was arrested!

Campbell also had very bad luck.

On the day of the eclipse, the sky was cloudy, and he could not see anything. The Russians took all his telescopes too, and he had to leave the Crimea.

In Berlin, Einstein could not believe his bad luck. He was very worried about what was going to happen to Freundlich. Finally, Freundlich was able to return to Germany, but the experiment was a failure.

America joined the war in 1917, but they were fighting against Germany. Einstein did not like the war at all, and he wanted to keep working with Campbell. But to Campbell, Einstein was a German, and the Germans were America's enemies.

The war was a difficult time for Einstein. His good friend Max Planck believed that the war was right, and so did another scientist named Fritz Haber. Haber was Einstein's boss, and Haber also helped him when he was having trouble with his wife. The two men were very good friends, but the things that Haber did in the war made Einstein very angry.

Einstein believed in peace and did not want to fight. When he looked out his window and saw the soldiers in the street going to fight the French and English, he thought they were crazy.

Haber was a great chemist, and he wanted to help Germany to win. He had an idea for a poison-gas weapon. Haber went to where the fighting was, and he used his new weapon to kill thousands of men.

Einstein believed that using science in this way was wrong. He was shocked that other scientists could use science to hurt or kill people.

Einstein decided to find other German scientists who did not like the war. But there were very few like him. He became a pacifist. There are many people like that today, but in Einstein's time, you had to be very brave to be one.

Einstein was alone, and his life was very difficult. It was a time of war, and it was difficult for Einstein to talk to scientists in other countries. But when he was alone, he had a chance to go back to his general theory of relativity. He looked at his old calculations.

One day, he looked at the old calculation about the way that light curves when it goes by the sun. And he saw that it was wrong! Now he was happy that Freundlich and Campbell had not been successful. If Einstein's calculations did not match the photos, no one would believe his theory. Photos of the eclipse might have ended his career.

In 1915, Einstein was asked to give a talk about his theory of general relativity. He was going to the Prussian Academy, a place where the greatest scientists went to meet. But there was no way to show that he was right, and there were mistakes in his math!

After eight years of thinking, Einstein was still not finished with his theory. He did not have much time. He worked night and day, doing more and more calculations. Another scientist might have given up, but not Einstein.

Another great thinker, David Hilbert, was also working on the theory of relativity. Einstein was very worried that Hilbert would find the answer before he did.

One day, Einstein went back to an old equation from three years before. It was a very good one, but at the time, he thought it was too strange. He started looking at it again, and somehow he knew that it was right.

Einstein also started thinking about an old mystery. He started thinking about the planet Mercury and the way it goes around the sun. Its orbit was strange, and this could not be explained by Newton's laws of gravity. Could Einstein use his equation to answer this very old question?

When Einstein used his calculations to understand the way Mercury moves around the sun, he saw that the match was almost perfect. Einstein's theory was right!

Both Einstein and Hilbert found the answer at about the same time. No one knows who was first. But Hilbert said that it was Einstein's theory, so he should be the winner.

On November 25, 1915, Albert Einstein gave his talk at the Prussian Academy. From that day on, it was no longer Newton's universe. It was Einstein's.

Einstein now knew that he was right, but he still needed proof from an eclipse. The war was still on, and there was not enough food in Germany.

Einstein became very sick in 1917, and his cousin Elsa came to take care of him. For the next three years, Einstein had many problems with his health.

Times were difficult, but something good also happened. Over the months, he became close to Elsa, and the two fell in love. Finally, they were married in 1919. She had two children already, Ilse and Margot, and the four of them became a family.

Elsa was very different from Mileva. She did not understand relativity at all! She was not interested in science, but she spoke French and English very well. She was a good translator and helper for Einstein. She loved to cook and clean for Einstein, and sometimes she was more like a mother than a wife.

Einstein and Eddington

At this time, there was a scientist in England named Arthur Eddington. He was an astronomer and also a pacifist like Einstein. Because of the war, it was very difficult for scientists to tell each other about their theories and work, but Eddington got a copy of one of Einstein's papers from a friend in the Netherlands.

When Eddington saw Einstein's theory of general relativity, he knew that he had to work on it. Eddington wanted to show that scientists in different countries could work together, even in a time of war. He was the only man in England who knew about it, and he knew it was his big chance.

The American astronomer William Campbell was now working to show that Einstein was wrong. He took pictures of an eclipse in America, and they did not support Einstein's theory. The problem was that he had lost his telescope in Russia, and he had to make a new one, but the parts were not very good.

The next eclipse was coming in June of 1918, but you could not see it in England. As soon as the war ended, Eddington went to Principe, a small island near Africa.

Eddington had to build a telescope in the middle of the jungle. On the day of the eclipse, the weather was cloudy, and it was very difficult to take pictures. Eddington did his best, but most of them were no good because of the clouds.

Finally, when he looked at the last pictures, Eddington saw that there were a few stars in them, and he hoped that he might be able to use them.

Eddington came back to England at the same time that Campbell was going to talk to the Royal Society. In his speech, Campbell said that Einstein was wrong, and showed them his photos. Many people believed him.

Almost at the end of his talk, though, someone came into the room carrying a telegram from Eddington. It said that he thought that Einstein might be right. Four months later, on November 6, 1919, Eddington gave his talk to the Royal Society.

When Eddington gave his talk, everyone was excited. He spoke in front of a picture of the great Isaac Newton. He pointed to the picture and said that he was sorry, but Newton was wrong! Eddington had found that Einstein was right!

Suddenly, Einstein became one of the most famous men in the world. Until that time, no one but scientists knew his name. People learned that everything that they believed about the universe was wrong!

It was a revolution in science. Few people were able to understand Einstein's ideas, but everyone knew his name. No one was more surprised by all of this than Einstein himself.

Suddenly, everyone wanted to talk

to Einstein, and he was asked by many people to go and speak to them. In 1921, Einstein was so popular that he was asked to go on a trip around the world. He went to the US, Britain, France, Japan, and Palestine.

When Einstein got to New York, people were very excited, and 15,000 men, women, and children came to see him. He traveled all over the country, and people loved him.

Einstein was popular, but there were still some scientists who did not believe his theories. People in America and England were still angry about the war, and many of them did not like Einstein because he was German.

Eddington's and Campbell's photos showed different things, so it was necessary to try again. The next chance to see an eclipse was coming in 1922. This eclipse was going to be in Australia.

Campbell went to Australia. He made a new telescope and went to a place called Ninety Mile Beach.

This time, Campbell was not alone. There were seven groups of scientists who went to Australia to see if Einstein was right! But because of the weather and other problems, most of the groups could not get good photos. Campbell was the only one who had success. He got photos of 92 stars.

Campbell very much wanted Einstein to be wrong. If he showed that Einstein made a mistake, Campbell would become very famous. But when he looked at the photos, he saw that the stars were in the places Einstein said they should be.

Campbell was a good scientist, and he had no choice but to tell everyone that Einstein's theory was right.

The war was now over, and people were very happy to have some good news. They were excited because a German Jew had worked with an English scientist while the two countries were at war. It seemed like the beginning of a new world.

The Greatest Scientist in the World

In 1922, Einstein won the Nobel Prize. As he promised, Einstein gave the money to Mileva.

Other scientists now began to use Einstein's ideas. In the same year, another man, Alexander Friedmann, used the theory of relativity in some very important work. Einstein said that the universe must either be getting bigger or getting smaller because if it did not, gravity would move all of the galaxies together.

Friedmann, a Russian mathematician, had an idea called the "big bang theory." The big bang theory says that the universe started from an explosion billions of years ago. It says that all the galaxies are moving away from each other very fast. His theory was only possible because of Einstein's work.

Later, in 1929, the famous astronomer Edwin Hubble showed that the universe really is getting bigger. Einstein had begun the new science of cosmology, the study of the universe.

Einstein had done many things in his life, but he was not even close to finished. In the 1920s, he started working to bring peace to the world. He wanted people to know about his pacifist ideas, and he joined the League of Nations' International Committee on Intellectual Cooperation. These men and women wanted to share science and culture from around the world to bring peace.

Einstein joined because he remembered the days during the war when he could not talk to other scientists. He believed that he had to do something to stop this kind of thing from happening again. When he saw the way that science had been used as a weapon during the war, he wanted to do something to make sure it was used only for peace.

During the 1920s, Einstein continued to travel all over. He was famous for his ideas, but he also became famous for the way he looked. Einstein did not like to brush his hair, and his clothes were usually old and worn. Often, he did not even wear socks. His strange hair became famous, and everywhere he went, people wanted to take his photo.

He was very busy giving speeches,

but Einstein also continued his scientific work. By the 1920s, most scientists knew that the old science of Newton did not work well with the world of atoms.

Physics had to change because of the work of Planck and Einstein.

After 1925, the world began to see a new quantum theory. Werner Heisenberg, Niels Bohr, and other men who made the theory said that there was no good way to predict what a particle will do.

Einstein did not like this idea at all. Why? Because Einstein believed that everything in the universe can be explained.

Einstein made calculations to explain matter and energy. He made calculations to explain gravity. Now he believed that there must also be a calculation to explain quantum particles. Einstein said, "[God] does not throw dice."

Einstein wanted to work on a "unified field theory." This theory would explain not just light and gravity, but also electrodynamics. Today, the laws of science that explain why airplanes can fly or how motors work are very different from the ones that explain the world of atoms. Einstein wanted one theory that could be used for everything.

In the days when Einstein first played with the compass he got from his father, he had the idea that everything in the world can be explained with fields. He really believed that he could find a way to bring everything in science together with one great theory.

Einstein worked and worked, and sometimes he thought that he was getting very close to the answer. But other scientists in the world thought that this time, his ideas were probably not right. They began to move on to other ideas, and once again, Einstein was almost alone.

At the Solvay Conferences of 1927 and 1930, Einstein argued with Niels Bohr from Denmark about the quantum theory. It went on day and night, and neither man gave up.

Today, most scientists think that Einstein was wrong in his hope of finding a unified field theory, but even when he was wrong, Einstein was a big help. In his debates with Niels Bohr and the other scientists who believed in the quantum theory, Einstein's criticisms were a big help in making them make their ideas better!

To America

In the early 1930s, Adolf Hitler and the Nazis were becoming more and more powerful in Germany. Einstein helped to make a group of Jews who tried to stop the Nazis during the 1920s, and the Nazis hated him.

Every day, things were getting much worse in Germany, and in 1932 Albert and Elsa went to America. While they were there, the Nazis took over the German government.

One of the first things the Nazis did was to make a law that said no Jews could work in any kind of official job. Einstein could not return to his job at the university. People were burning books written by Jews, and Einstein was being attacked all the time.

Then the Nazis did something more shocking. They said that they would give $5,000 to the person who killed Einstein. It was too dangerous for him to go back to Germany because he was a Jew.

Einstein decided to stay in America. He was asked to come to the famous Princeton University, and he and Elsa bought a house in Princeton, New Jersey in 1935.

Sadly, though, Elsa died the very next

year. She had taken care of Einstein for many years, but now he was alone. He found a secretary to help him, and one of Elsa's daughters came to live with him in Princeton.

During these years, Einstein tried to finish his unified field theory. Since his debates with Niels Bohr, Einstein had seen that quantum physics was good for understanding the way that atoms worked. Using it, science was able to explain almost everything that happened in the physical world. But he still thought it was possible to find a better theory.

Einstein still wanted to work by himself, but all around the world, scientists were starting to work in bigger and bigger groups. People like Einstein who wanted to do theory were working together with scientists in labs. They were getting a lot of money from the government, and they were using expensive technology to do their experiments.

Einstein was still a genius, but science had changed, and he was just one man. He could not keep up. Einstein never stopped working on his theories, but after the 1920s, he was much more important as a man who worked to change society than he was as a scientist.

In the late 1930s, Einstein saw the Nazis becoming stronger and more dangerous. He saw the terrible things they were doing to Jews in Germany. The Nazis were taking the Jews' money and houses, and making them leave the country. Einstein helped as many Jews as he could to come to America.

The things he saw in Germany made Einstein change his mind about war. He now thought that Hitler and Germany were so dangerous that there was no choice but to attack them.

In 1939, a scientist from Hungary named Leo Szilard told Einstein that the Germans were working to make an atom bomb.

Einstein did not know much about the atom bomb, so Szilard explained it to him. He told Einstein about how powerful it was, and the great dangers of these weapons.

Einstein was very worried, and he believed that if Hitler had a weapon like that, it would be a terrible thing. He wrote a letter to the American president

To America

Albert Einstein
Old Grove Rd.
Nassau Point
Peconic, Long Island

August 2nd, 1939

F. D. Roosevelt
President of the United States,
White House
Washington, D.C.

Sir:

Recent work in nuclear physics made it probable that uranium may be turned into a new and important source of energy. New experiments performed by E.Fermi and L.Szilard, which have been communicated to me in manuscript, make it now appear likely that it will be possible to set up a chain reaction in a large mass of uranium and thereby to liberate considerable quantities of energy. Less certain, but to be kept in mind, is the possibility of making use of such chain reactions for the construction of extremely powerful bombs. Such bombs may be too heavy for transportation by air plane, but not too heavy for being carried by boat, and a single bomb exploded in a port might very well destroy the port together with the surrounding territory.

This being the situation, you may find it desirable that some contact be established between the Administration and the group of physicists who are working in this country on the subject of chain reactions. One possible way of achieving this would be for you to entrust a person who has your

Einstein's letter to Roosevelt

Franklin Delano Roosevelt. Einstein told him that America should make its own atom bomb and do everything it could to stop Hitler.

Einstein was the most famous scientist in the world, and when he talked, people listened. If he had never written that letter, no one knows if America would have made the atom bomb or not.

America started the Manhattan Project and began making the world's first atom bomb.

The war years were a difficult time for Einstein. He still had many friends in Germany, and it was still a country that he loved. He did not like the Nazis, but it was terrible to see fighting in such a beautiful place and to hear of friends dying.

Einstein wanted to help America, so he helped the government to get money. He sold many of his famous papers. His paper on special relativity from 1905 was sold for $6.5 million!

The Manhattan Project thought about asking Einstein to help, but there was a problem. He was a German, and he was a member of some socialist groups.

Einstein never did any work on the atom bomb, and in the end, he was glad that he did not. In August of 1945, America used atom bombs on the cities of Hiroshima and Nagasaki in Japan.

At the end of the war, Einstein was happy that the danger from Germany and Japan was over, but he also felt very sad. When Einstein heard about the terrible power of the atom bomb and how many people it killed, he wished that he had never told Roosevelt to make it.

In his later years after the war was finished, Einstein was very afraid of the danger of nuclear weapons. He watched as the United States and Russia built more and more of them. Einstein wanted to do something, and he often spoke about the dangers of nuclear war.

Einstein also started working to make society better in other ways. He supported the black rights movement, and he asked America and England to make a homeland for Jews in Israel.

In 1952, the new country of Israel asked Einstein to be its first president! He did not take the job, but many people think he would have been a very good one.

Einstein's Last Days

By the year 1955, Einstein knew that he was going to die soon. He had a serious heart problem, and it was getting worse. He looked back over his whole life, thinking about all the things he had done.

In this last year of his life, Einstein wanted to do something for peace. He talked to his old friend, the famous philosopher Bertrand Russell. They were both very afraid of the power of nuclear weapons, and they wanted to do something to make the world safer.

Einstein and Russell decided that they should get scientists to come together to sign a document calling for peace and an end to nuclear weapons.

This was the beginning of the Pugwash Conferences where scientists get together to talk about nuclear weapons and other problems, and to work for peace. They are still very important today.

On April 12, 1955, Einstein went in to work, but he was in terrible pain. Someone asked him, "Is everything all right?" He answered, "Everything is all right, but I am not."

Einstein stayed at home on the 13th. In the afternoon, he became even worse. The night was long and difficult, and the next day, a group of doctors came to his home. They told him that he had to go to hospital. Einstein did not want to go, but in the end, he had no choice.

Einstein was a scientist until the very

end. Even when he was dying, the only things that he asked for were his glasses, a pen, and his equations.

Einstein knew that he did not have

Einstein in his study near the end of his life

much more time, and the only thing that he wanted was to finish the unified field theory.

His body was becoming weaker and weaker, but Einstein kept working. Sometimes he fell asleep, but as soon as he woke up, he picked up his pen and went back to work. He hoped that this would be his greatest theory.

Einstein had been working on his theory for more than 30 years, but he did not have any more time.

A little after 1 A.M. on April 18, 1955, Einstein said a few words in German and died.

Since Einstein died, he has only become more famous and important. Today, Einstein is everywhere. He is in books, he is in movies, and he is on

T-shirts. But most of all, he is in our science and the things we use every day.

When we use a GPS, we need his theory of general relativity for the calculations. We also use general relativity when we calculate how satellites move.

Einstein's ideas gave us lasers and nuclear energy. He helped us to find black holes and showed us that the universe is getting bigger and bigger.

We use Einstein's famous equation, $E=mc^2$, to calculate nuclear energy, to do PET scans in hospitals, and much, much more.

Most of the work that scientists are doing in physics today is based on his work. In the future, Einstein's theory of general relativity may even help us travel to the stars.

Word List

- 本文で使われている全ての語を掲載しています（LEVEL 1, 2）。ただし、LEVEL 3以上は、中学校レベルの語を含みません。
- 語形が規則変化する語の見出しは原形で示しています。不規則変化語は本文中で使われている形になっています。
- 一般的な意味を紹介していますので、一部の語で本文中で実際に使われている品詞や意味と合っていないことがあります。
- 品詞は以下のように示しています。

名 名詞	代 代名詞	形 形容詞	副 副詞	動 動詞	助 助動詞
前 前置詞	接 接続詞	間 間投詞	冠 冠詞	略 略語	俗 俗語
頭 接頭語	尾 接尾語	房 記号	関 関係代名詞		

A

- **a** 冠 ①1つの, 1人の, ある ②〜につき
- **Aarau** 名 アーラウ《地名, スイスのアールガウ自治州の州都》
- **Aaron Bernstein** アーロン・ベルンシュタイン《ドイツ系ユダヤ人の科学者で著作家, 1812-1884》
- **able** 形 ①《be – to ~》(人が)〜することができる ②能力のある
- **about** 副 ①およそ, 約 ②まわりに, あたりを be about to まさに〜しようとしている, 〜するところだ 前 ①〜について ②〜のまわりに[の]
- **academy** 名 ①アカデミー, 学士院 ②学園, 学院
- **accelerate** 動 加速する
- **acceleration** 名 加速, 加速度
- **across** 前 〜を渡って, 〜の向こう側に
- **actually** 副 実際に, 本当に, 実は
- **Adolf Hitler** アドルフ・ヒトラー《ドイツの政治家, 国家社会主義ドイツ労働者党党首として, 反ユダヤ主義を掲げる。1939年のポーランド侵攻によって第二次世界大戦を引き起こした。1889-1945》
- **adult** 名 大人, 成人
- **affect** 動 影響する
- **afraid** 形 ①心配して ②恐れて, こわがって
- **Africa** 名 アフリカ《大陸》
- **after** 前 ①〜の後に[で], 〜の次に ②《前後に名詞がきて》次々に〜, 何度も〜《反復・継続を表す》副 後に[で] 接 (〜した)後に[で]
- **afternoon** 名 午後
- **again** 副 再び, もう一度 again and again 何度も繰り返して
- **against** 前 ①〜に対して, 〜に反対して
- **age** 名 年齢 at the age of 〜歳のときに
- **ago** 副 〜前に
- **airplane** 名 飛行機
- **Albert Einstein** アルベルト・アインシュタイン《ドイツ生まれのユダヤ人理論物理学者, 1879-1955》
- **Alexander Friedmann** アレクサンドル・フリードマン《ソ連の宇宙物理学者, 1922年に一般相対性理論の場の方程式に従う膨張宇宙のモデルをフリードマン方程式の解として定式化したことで知られる。1888-1925》

Word List

- **all** 形すべての, ~中 **all the time** ずっと, いつも, その間ずっと 代全部, すべて(のもの[人]) **most of all** とりわけ, 中でも **not ~ at all** 少しも[全然]~ない 名全体 **all over** ~中で, 全体に亘って **all right** 大丈夫で, よろしい, 申し分ない 副まったく, すっかり

- **almost** 副ほとんど, もう少しで(~するところ)

- **alone** 形ただひとりの 副ひとりで, ~だけで

- **already** 副すでに, もう

- **also** 副~も(また), ~も同様に

- **always** 副いつも, 常に

- **am** 動~である, (~に)いる[ある] 《主語がIのときのbeの現在形》

- **A.M.** 略午前

- **ambitious** 形大望のある, 野心的な

- **America** 名アメリカ《国名・大陸》

- **American** 形アメリカ(人)の 名アメリカ人

- **amount** 名量

- **an** 冠①1つの, 1人の, ある ②~につき

- **and** 接①そして, ~と… ②《同じ語を結んで》ますます ③《結果を表して》それで, だから

- **angle** 名①角度 ②角

- **angry** 形怒って, 腹を立てて **get angry** 腹を立てる

- **Annalen Der Physik** 『物理学年報』《ドイツの学術誌. 最も有名でかつ歴史ある物理ジャーナルとして知られる. 1780~》

- **another** 形①もう1つ[1人]の ②別の

- **answer** 動①答える, 応じる ②《-for ~》~の責任を負う 名答え, 応答, 返事

- **any** 形①《疑問文で》何か, いくつかの ②《否定文で》何も, 少しも(~ない) ③《肯定文で》どの~も 代①《疑問文で》《~のうち》何か, 誰か ②《否定文で》少しも, 何も[誰も]~ない ③《肯定文で》どれも, 誰でも

- **anything** 代①《疑問文で》何か, どれでも ②《否定文で》何も, どれも(~ない) ③《肯定文で》何でも, どれでも 副いくらか

- **anywhere** 副どこかへ[に], どこにも, どこへも, どこにでも

- **apple** 名リンゴ

- **April** 名4月

- **are** 動~である, (~に)いる[ある] 《主語がyou, we, theyまたは複数名詞のときのbeの現在形》

- **area** 名地域, 地方, 区域, 場所

- **argue** 動論じる, 議論する

- **around** 副まわりに, あちこちに **go around** 動き回る, あちらこちらに行く, 回り道をする, (障害)を回避する **move around** ~の周りを移動する **walk around** 歩き回る, ぶらぶら歩く 前~のまわりに, ~のあちこちに

- **arrest** 動逮捕する

- **arrive** 動到着する, 到達する **arrive in** ~に着く

- **Arthur Eddington** アーサー・エディントン《イギリスの天文学者. 相対性理論に関する業績で知られる. アインシュタインの一般相対性理論を英語圏に紹介した. 1882-1944》

- **as** 接①《as ~ as …の形で》…と同じくらい ②~のとおりに, ~のように ③~しながら, ~しているときに ④~するにつれて, ~にしたがって ⑤~なので ⑥~だけども ⑦~する限りでは 前①~として(の) ②~の時 **as if** あたかも~のように, まるで~みたいに **as though** あたかも~のように, まるで~みたいに **as you know** ご存知のとおり 副同じくらい **as ~ as one can** できる限り~ **as soon as** ~するとすぐ, ~す

THE ALBERT EINSTEIN STORY

るや否や 代 ①〜のような ②〜だが
- **ask** 動 ①尋ねる, 聞く ②頼む, 求める ask 〜 if 〜かどうか尋ねる
- **asleep** 副 眠って fall asleep 眠り込む, 寝入る
- **assistant** 名 助手, 補佐
- **astronomer** 名 天文学者
- **at** 前 ①《場所・時》〜に[で] ②《目標・方向》〜に[を], 〜に向かって ③《原因・理由》〜を見て[聞いて・知って] ④〜に従事して, 〜の状態で
- **atom** 名 原子 atom bomb 原子爆弾
- **attack** 動 ①襲う, 攻める ②非難する
- **August** 名 8月
- **Australia** 名 オーストラリア《国名》
- **away** 副 離れて, 遠くに, 去って, わきに from far away 遠くから move away from 〜から遠ざかる

B

- **baby** 名 赤ん坊
- **back** 名 ①背中 ②裏, 後ろ 副 ①戻って ②後ろへ[に] come back to 〜へ帰ってくる, 〜に戻る go back to 〜に帰る[戻る], 〜に遡る, (中断していた作業に)再び取り掛かる look back at 〜に視線を戻す, 〜を振り返って見る
- **bad** 形 悪い, へたな, まずい bad luck 災難, 不運, 悪運
- **ball** 名 ボール, 球
- **bang** 名 衝撃音, 銃声, バン[ドスン・バタン]という音 動 ドスンと鳴る, 強く打つ
- **bankrupt** 形 破産した, 支払い能力のない go bankrupt 破産する
- **based** 形 〜に拠点のある, 〜をベース[基礎]にした be based on 〜に基づく
- **be** 動 〜である, (〜に)いる[ある], 〜となる 助 ①《現在分詞とともに用いて》〜している ②《過去分詞とともに用いて》〜される, 〜されている
- **beach** 名 海辺, 浜
- **beam** 名 光線
- **beautiful** 形 美しい, すばらしい
- **beauty** 名 ①美, 美しい人[物] ②《the –》美点
- **became** 動 become (なる)の過去
- **because** 接 (なぜなら)〜だから, 〜という理由[原因]で because of 〜のために, 〜の理由で
- **become** 動 ①(〜に)なる ②(〜に)似合う ③become の過去分詞
- **bed** 名 ベッド, 寝所 be sick in bed 病気で寝ている
- **been** 動 be (〜である)の過去分詞 助 be (〜している・〜される)の過去分詞
- **before** 前 〜の前に[で], 〜より以前に 接 〜する前に 副 以前に
- **began** 動 begin (始まる)の過去
- **begin** 動 始まる[始める], 起こる
- **beginning** 動 begin (始まる)の現在分詞 名 初め, 始まり
- **begun** 動 begin (始まる)の過去分詞
- **behind** 前 〜の後ろに, 〜の背後に 副 後ろに, 背後に
- **believe** 動 信じる, 信じている, (〜と)思う, 考える believe in 〜を信じる
- **Berlin** 名 ベルリン《ドイツ連邦共和国の首都》
- **Berlin Observatory** ベルリン天文台《ベルリン郊外に建てられたが, 1913にポツダムに移設. 1700–》
- **Bern** 名 ベルン《スイス連邦の首都》
- **Bernstein, Aaron** アーロン・ベルンシュタイン《ドイツ系ユダヤ人の

科学者で著作家。1812-1884》
- **Bertrand Russell** バートランド・ラッセル《イギリス生まれの論理学者、数学者、哲学者。1872-1970》
- **beside** 前 ～のそばに、～と並んで
- **best** 形 最もよい、最大[多]の do one's best 全力を尽くす 副 最もよく、最も上手に 名《the -》①最上のもの ②全力、精いっぱい
- **better** 形 ①よりよい ②(人が)回復して feel better 気分がよくなる 副 ①よりよく、より上手に ②むしろ
- **big** 形 ①大きい ②偉い、重要な 副 ①大きく、大いに ②自慢して
- **big bang** ビッグバン、宇宙大爆発
- **billion** 名 10億
- **black** 形 黒い、有色の 名 黒、黒色
- **black hole** ブラックホール
- **black rights movement** 公民権運動《1950年代から1960年代にかけてアメリカの黒人が公民権の適用と人種差別の解消を求めて行った大衆運動》
- **block** 名 ブロック、つみ木
- **blue** 形 青い 名 青(色)
- **body** 名 体
- **Bohr, Niels** ニールス・ボーア《デンマークの理論物理学者。量子力学の確立に貢献。量子力学に反対するアインシュタインと論争を続けた。1885-1962》
- **bomb** 名 爆弾
- **book** 名 本、書物
- **born** 動 be born 生まれる
- **boss** 名 上司、親方、監督
- **both** 形 両方の、2つともの 副《both ～ and … の形で》～も…も両方とも 代 両方、両者、双方
- **bought** 動 buy(買う)の過去、過去分詞
- **boy** 名 少年、男の子
- **brave** 形 勇敢な
- **bright** 形 利口な
- **bring** 動 ①持ってくる、連れてくる ②もたらす、生じる
- **Britain** 名 英国
- **brother** 名 兄弟
- **brush** 動 ブラシをかける
- **build** 動 建てる
- **built** 動 build(建てる)の過去、過去分詞
- **bullet** 名 銃弾、弾丸状のもの
- **burn** 動 燃える、燃やす
- **bus** 名 バス
- **busy** 形 忙しい
- **but** 接 ①でも、しかし ②～を除いて have no choice but to ～するしかない not ～ but … ～ではなくて… 前 ～を除いて、～のほかは 副 ただ、のみ、ほんの
- **by** 前 ①《位置》～のそばに[で] ②《手段・方法・行為者・基準》～によって、～で ③《期限》～までには ④《通過・経由》～を経由して、～を通って 副 そばに、通り過ぎて

C

- **C** 略 光速度《光が伝播する速さ。真空中における光速の値は約30万キロメートル毎秒。ラテン語で速さを意味するceleritasの頭文字》
- **calculate** 動 ①計算する、算出する ②見積もる、予想する
- **calculation** 名 計算、勘定、見積もり
- **call** 動 呼ぶ、叫ぶ call for ～を求める、訴える、～を呼び求める、呼び出す
- **came** 動 come(来る)の過去
- **Campbell, William Wallace** ウィリアム・キャンベル《アメリカ合衆国の天文学者。1862-1938》
- **can** 助 ①～できる ②～してもよい

(3)〜でありうる (4)《否定文で》〜のはずがない as 〜 as one can できる限り〜
- **cannot** can(〜できる)の否定形(=can not)
- **card** 名 トランプ
- **care** 名 世話, 介護 take care of 〜 の世話をする, 〜面倒を見る, 〜を管理する
- **career** 名 ①(生涯の・専門的な)職業 ②経歴, キャリア
- **carry** 動 ①運ぶ, 連れていく, 持ち歩く ②伝わる, 伝える
- **case** 名 実例, 場合, 実状, 状況
- **catch** 動 ①つかまえる ②追いつく catch up to 〜に追いつく
- **cause** 動 〜の原因になる, 〜を引き起こす《be》caused by 〜に起因する
- **center** 名 ①中心, 中央 ②中心地[人物]
- **chair** 名 いす
- **chance** 名 ①偶然, 運 ②好機
- **change** 動 変わる, 変える 名 変化, 変更
- **check** 動 照合する, 検査する
- **chemist** 名 化学者
- **child** 名 子ども
- **children** 名 child(子ども)の複数
- **choice** 名 選択(の範囲・自由) have no choice but to 〜するしかない
- **city** 名 都市, 都会
- **class** 名 授業
- **clean** 動 掃除する
- **clerk** 名 事務員 patent clerk 特許審査官
- **clock** 名 掛け[置き]時計
- **close** 形 ①近い ②親しい ③狭い be close to 〜に近い get close to 〜に近づく, 接近する 動 ①閉まる, 閉める ②終える, 閉店する close down 閉店する, 廃業する
- **cloth** 名 布(地)
- **clothes** 名 衣服, 身につけるもの
- **cloud** 名 雲, 雲状のもの, 煙
- **cloudy** 形 曇った, 雲の多い
- **club** 名 クラブ, (同好)会
- **color** 名 色, 色彩
- **come** 動 ①来る, 行く, 現れる ②(出来事が)起こる, 生じる ③〜になる ④comeの過去分詞 come back to 〜へ帰ってくる, 〜に戻る come in やってくる come into 〜に入ってくる come out of 〜から出てくる dream come true 夢がかなった
- **committee** 名 評議会, 委員(会), 受託人
- **company** 名 会社
- **compass** 名 羅針盤, 方位磁石
- **conference** 名 ①会議, 協議, 相談 ②協議会
- **continue** 動 続く, 続ける
- **cook** 動 料理する
- **cooperation** 名 協力, 協業, 協調
- **copy** 名 コピー, 写し
- **cosmology** 名 宇宙論
- **could** 助 ①can(〜できる)の過去 ②《控え目な推量・可能性・願望などを表す》could have done 〜だったかもしれない《仮定法》If +《主語》+ could 〜できればなあ《仮定法》
- **country** 名 国
- **course** 名 of course もちろん, 当然
- **cousin** 名 いとこ
- **crazy** 形 ①狂気の, ばかげた, 無茶な ②夢中の, 熱狂的な
- **creative** 形 創造力のある, 独創的な
- **creativity** 名 創造性, 独創力
- **Crimea** 名 クリミア半島《黒海の北岸, ウクライナにある半島》

WORD LIST

- **criticism** 名 批評, 非難, 反論, 評論
- **cry** 動 泣く, 叫ぶ, 大声を出す, 嘆く
- **culture** 名 ①文化 ②教養
- **curve** 動 曲がる, 曲げる
- **curved** 形 湾曲した, 曲線状の

D

- **danger** 名 危険, 障害, 脅威
- **dangerous** 形 危険な, 有害な
- **daughter** 名 娘
- **David Hilbert** ダフィット・ヒルベルト《ドイツの数学者, 1862-1943》
- **day** 名 ①日中, 昼間 ②日, 期日 ③《-s》時代, 生涯 day and night 昼も夜も every day 毎日 for days and days くる日もくる日も in those days あのころは, 当時は one day (過去の)ある日, (未来の)いつか
- **debate** 名 討論, ディベート
- **decide** 動 決定[決意]する, (~しようと)決める, 判決を下す decide to do ~することに決める
- **declare** 動 宣言する
- **deeply** 副 深く, 非常に
- **Denmark** 名 デンマーク《国名》
- **dice** 名 さいころ, ダイス
- **did** 動 do(~をする)の過去 助 do の過去
- **die** 動 死ぬ, 消滅する
- **different** 形 異なった, 違った, 別の, さまざまな be different from ~と違う
- **difficult** 形 困難な, むずかしい, 扱いにくい
- **direction** 名 ①方向, 方角 ②《-s》指示, 説明書 ③指導, 指揮
- **divorce** 名 離婚, 分異
- **do** 動 ①《ほかの動詞とともに用いて現在形の否定文・疑問文をつくる》②《同じ動詞を繰り返す代わりに用いる》③《動詞を強調するのに用いる》動 ~をする
- **doctor** 名 医者, 博士(号)
- **document** 名 文書, 記録 動 (~を)記録する
- **does** 動 do(~をする)の3人称単数現在 助 do の3人称単数現在
- **$** 略 ドル, 米国の貨幣単位
- **done** 動 do(~をする)の過去分詞
- **down** 副 ①下へ, 降りて, 低くなって ②倒れて 前 ~の下方へ, ~をドって
- **dream** 名 夢, 幻想 dream come true 夢がかなった 動 (~の)夢を見る, 夢想[想像]する dream of ~を夢見る
- **dreamer** 名 夢を見る人, 夢想家
- **during** 前 ~の間(ずっと)
- **dust** 名 ちり, ほこり, ごみ, 粉 dust particle 塵状の個体粒子 動 ちり[ほこり]を払う
- **dying** 動 die(死ぬ)の現在分詞 形 死にかかっている, 消えそうな

E

- **E** 略 エネルギー《energy の頭文字》
- **E=mc^2** アルベルト・アインシュタインが特殊相対性理論の帰結として発表した有名な関係式。質量とエネルギーの等価性とも言われる。
- **each other** お互いに
- **early** 形 ①(時間や時期が)早い ②初期の, 幼少の, 若い
- **earth** 名 ①《the -》地球 ②大地, 陸地, 土 ③この世 on earth 地球上で, この世で
- **easy** 形 ①やさしい, 簡単な ②気楽な, くつろいだ
- **eclipse** 名 日食
- **Eddington, Arthur** アーサー・

THE ALBERT EINSTEIN STORY

エディントン《イギリスの天文学者. 相対性理論に関する業績で知られる。アインシュタインの一般相対性理論を英語圏に紹介した。1882-1944》

- **Eduard** 名 エドゥアルト《アインシュタインの次男, 1910-1965》
- **Edwin Hubble** エドウィン・ハッブル《アメリカ合衆国の天文学者. 現代の宇宙論の基礎を築いた。1889-1953》
- **effect** 名 影響, 効果, 結果
- **Eidgenössische Technische Hochschule** スイス連邦工科大学《スイスにある工学系の単科大学, 1855-》
- **eight** 名 8(の数字), 8人[個] 形 8の, 8人[個]の
- **Einstein** 名 ①アルベルト・アインシュタイン《ドイツ生まれのユダヤ人理論物理学者, 1879-1955》②アインシュタイン《名字》
- **either** 形 ①(2つのうち)どちらかの ②どちらでも 代 どちらでも ①どちらか ②《否定文で》~もまた(…ない) 接《- ~ or …》~かまたは…か
- **electric** 形 電気の, 電動の
- **electricity** 名 電気
- **electrodynamics** 名 電気力学
- **elevator** 名 エレベーター
- **Elsa** 名 エルザ《アインシュタインのいとこで2番目の妻, 1876-1936》
- **else** 副 ①そのほかに[の], 代わりに ②さもないと
- **end** 名 ①終わり, 終末, 死 ②果て, 末, 端 ③目的 at the end of ~の終わりに in the end とうとう, ついに very end 最後の最後 動 終わる, 終える
- **enemy** 名 敵
- **energy** 名 エネルギー
- **engineer** 名 技師
- **England** 名 ①イングランド ②英国
- **English** 名 ①英語 ②《the - 》英国人 形 ①英語の ②英国(人)の
- **enjoy** 動 楽しむ, 享受する enjoy doing ~するのが好きだ, ~するのを楽しむ
- **enough** 形 十分な, (~するに)足る 名 十分(な量・数), たくさん 副 (~できる)だけ, 十分に, まったく
- **enter** 動 入る, 入会[入学]する[させる]
- **equation** 名 方程式
- **Erwin Finlay-Freundlich** エルヴィン・フィンレイ=フロイントリッヒ《ドイツ人天文学者. アインシュタインの一般相対性理論を検証するために, 1914年, 8月21日の日食を観測するために遠征隊を率いてクリミア半島に向かった。1885-1964》
- **Euclid** 名 ユークリッド原論《紀元前3世紀ごろにエジプトのアレクサンドリアで活躍した数学者エウクレイデス(ユークリッド)によって編纂された数学書》
- **Europe** 名 ヨーロッパ
- **even** 副 ①《強意》~でさえも, ~ですら, いっそう, なおさら ②平等に even if たとえ~でも 形 ①平らな, 水平の ②等しい, 均一の ③落ち着いた
- **ever** 副 ①今までに, これまで, かつて, いつまでも ②《強意》いったい
- **every** 形 ①どの~も, すべての, あらゆる ②毎~, ~ごとの every day 毎日
- **everyone** 代 誰でも, 皆
- **everything** 代 すべてのこと[もの], 何でも, 何もかも
- **everywhere** 副 どこにいても, いたるところに
- **excellent** 形 優れた, 優秀な
- **excited** 動 excite(興奮する)の過去, 過去分詞 形 興奮した, わくわくした
- **exciting** 形 興奮させる, わくわく

- □ **expensive** 形 高価な, ぜいたくな
- □ **experiment** 名 実験, 試み thought experiment 思考実験
- □ **explain** 動 説明する, 明らかにする, 釈明[弁明]する
- □ **explosion** 名 爆発

F

- □ **fabric** 名 ①織物, 生地 ②構造
- □ **face** 名 顔, 顔つき face to face 面と向かって
- □ **fail** 動 失敗する, 落第する[させる]
- □ **failure** 名 ①失敗, 落第 ②不足, 欠乏 ③停止, 減退
- □ **fall** 動 ①落ちる, 倒れる ②(値段・温度が)下がる ③(ある状態に)急に陥る fall asleep 眠り込む, 寝入る fall down 落ちる, 転ぶ fall in love with 恋におちる fall off 落ちる, 落ち込む, 下落する, 減る, 衰退する 名 ①落下, 墜落 ②滝 ③崩壊 ④秋
- □ **family** 名 家族, 家庭, 一門, 家柄
- □ **famous** 形 有名な, 名高い be famous for ～で有名である
- □ **far** 副 ①遠くに, はるかに, 離れて ②《比較級を強めて》ずっと, はるかに from far away 遠くから
- □ **fast** 形 ①(速度が)速い ②(時計が)進んでいる ③しっかりした 副 ①速く, 急いで ②(時計が)進んで ③しっかりと, ぐっすりと
- □ **fast-moving** 形 動きの速い
- □ **father** 名 父親
- □ **favorite** 形 お気に入りの, ひいきの
- □ **feel** 動 感じる, (～と)思う feel better 気分がよくなる
- □ **fell** 動 fall (落ちる)の過去
- □ **felt** 動 feel (感じる)の過去, 過去分詞
- □ **few** 形 ①ほとんどない, 少数の(～しかない) ②《a-》少数の, 少しはある
- □ **field** 名 野原, 田畑, 広がり unified field theory 統一場理論
- □ **fight** 動 (～と)戦う, 争う 名 ①戦い, 争い, けんか ②闘志, ファイト
- □ **fighting** 名 戦闘
- □ **finally** 副 最後に, ついに, 結局
- □ **find** 動 ①見つける ②(～と)わかる, 気づく, ～と考える ③得る
- □ **finish** 動 終わる, 終える
- □ **first** 名 最初, 第一(の人・物) at first 最初は, 初めのうちは 形 ①第一の, 最初の ②最も重要な 副 第一に, 最初に
- □ **five** 名 5(の数字), 5人[個] 形 5の, 5人[個]の
- □ **float** 動 浮く, 浮かぶ
- □ **flower** 名 花, 草花
- □ **fly** 動 飛ぶ, 飛ばす
- □ **food** 名 食物
- □ **for** 前 ①《目的・原因・対象》～にとって, ～のために[の], ～に対して ②《期間》～間 ③《代理》～の代わりに ④《方向》～へ(向かって) 接 というわけは～, なぜなら～, だから
- □ **force** 名 力, 勢い
- □ **forever** 副 永遠に, 絶えず
- □ **found** 動 find (見つける)の過去, 過去分詞
- □ **four** 名 4(の数字), 4人[個] 形 4の, 4人[個]の
- □ **France** 名 フランス《国名》
- □ **Franklin Delano Roosevelt** フランクリン・ルーズベルト《アメリカ合衆国の政治家, 第32代アメリカ大統領, 任期1933-1945》
- □ **free** 形 自由な, 開放された, 自由に～できる
- □ **French** 形 フランス(人・語)の 名 ①フランス語 ②《the-》フラン

ス人

- **Freundlich, Erwin Finlay-** エルヴィン・フィンレイ＝フロイントリッヒ《ドイツ人天文学者。アインシュタインの一般相対性理論を検証するために、1914年、8月21日の日食を観測するために遠征隊を率いてクリミア半島に向かった。1885-1964》

- **Friedmann, Alexander** アレクサンドル・フリードマン《ソ連の宇宙物理学者。1922年に一般相対性理論の場の方程式に従う膨張宇宙モデルをフリードマン方程式の解として定式化したことで知られる。1888-1925》

- **friend** 名 友だち、仲間

- **friendly** 形 親しみのある、親切な、友情のこもった

- **Fritz Haber** フリッツ・ハーバー《ドイツ出身の物理化学者。化学兵器の父とも呼ばれる。1868-1934》

- **from** 前 ①《出身・出発点・時間・順序・原料》～から ②《原因・理由》～がもとで from ～ to … ～から…まで

- **front** 名 正面、前 in front of ～の前に、～の正面に 形 正面の、前面の

- **fuel** 名 燃料

- **full** 形 ①満ちた、いっぱいの、満期の ②完全な、盛りの、充実した

- **fun** 名 楽しみ、冗談、おもしろいこと

- **future** 名 未来、将来 in the future 将来は 形 未来の、将来の

G

- **galaxy** 名 ①《the -, the G-》星雲、銀河 ②《the G-》銀河系
- **game** 名 ゲーム、試合、遊び、競技
- **gave** 動 give (与える) の過去
- **general** 形 全体の、一般の、普通の
- **general (theory of) relativity** 一般相対性理論
- **genius** 名 天才、才能
- **gentlemen** 名 gentleman (紳士) の複数
- **German** 形 ドイツ(人・語)の 名 ①ドイツ人 ②ドイツ語
- **Germany** 名 ドイツ《国名》
- **get** 動 ①得る、手に入れる ②(ある状態に)なる、いたる ③わかる、理解する ④～させる、～を(…の状態に)する ⑤(ある場所に)達する、着く get a job 職を得る get angry 腹を立てる get close to ～に近づく、接近する get off (～から) 降りる get smaller 小さくなる get someone to do (人) に～させる[してもらう] get to (事) を始める、～に達する[到着する] get worse 悪化する
- **girl** 名 女の子、少女
- **girlfriend** 名 女友だち
- **give** 動 ①与える、贈る ②伝える、述べる ③(～を) する give up あきらめる、やめる、引き渡す
- **given** 動 give (与える) の過去分詞 形 与えられた
- **glad** 形 ①うれしい、喜ばしい ②《be - to ～》～してうれしい、喜んで～する
- **glass** 名 《-es》めがね
- **go** 動 ①行く、出かける ②動く ③進む、経過する、いたる ④(ある状態に) なる be going to ～するつもりである go and ～しに行く go against (常識・規則などに) 逆らう、反する go around 動き回る、あちらこちらに行く、回り道をする、(障害)を回避する go back to ～に帰る[戻る]、～に遡る、(中断していた作業に) 再び取り掛かる go by ①(時が) 過ぎる、経過する ②～のそばを通る ③～に基づいて[よって] 行う go in (仕事を) 始める go into 出版される go on 続く、続ける、進み続ける、起こる、発生する go on a trip 旅行する go out 外へ出る go up ①～に上がる、

登る ②～に近づく, 出かける
- **God** 名 神
- **good** 形 ①よい, 上手な, 優れた, 美しい ②(数量・程度が)かなりの, 相当な　be good at ～が得意だ
- **goodbye** 間 さようなら 名 別れのあいさつ
- **got** 動 get (得る)の過去, 過去分詞
- **government** 名 政治, 政府
- **GPS** 略 グローバル・ポジショニング・システム《global positioning systemの略》
- **gravity** 名 重力, 引力
- **great** 形 ①大きい, 広大な, (量や程度が)たいへんな ②偉大な, 優れた ③すばらしい, おもしろい
- **green** 名 緑色
- **Grossmann, Marcel** マルセル・グロスマン《ハンガリー出身の数学者。アインシュタインに, 一般相対性理論の発展に対するリーマン幾何学の必要性を説いた。1878-1936》
- **ground** 名 地面, 土, 土地
- **group** 名 集団, 群 動 集まる

H

- **Haber, Fritz** フリッツ・ハーバー《ドイツ出身の物理化学学者。化学兵器の父とも呼ばれる。1868-1934》
- **had** 動 have (持つ)の過去, 過去分詞 助 haveの過去《過去完了の文をつくる》
- **hair** 名 髪, 毛
- **hand** 名 ①手 ②(時計の)針
- **Hans Albert** ハンス・アルベルト《アインシュタインの長男, カリフォルニア大学バークレー校教授。1904-1973》
- **happen** 動 ①(出来事が)起こる, 生じる ②偶然[たまたま]～する
- **happy** 形 幸せな, うれしい, 幸運な, 満足して　be happy to do ～してうれしい, 喜んで～する
- **hard** 形 ①堅い ②激しい, むずかしい ③熱心な, 勤勉な ④無情な, 耐えがたい, 厳しい, きつい
- **has** 動 have (持つ)の3人称単数現在 助 haveの3人称単数現在《現在完了の文をつくる》
- **hate** 動 嫌う, 憎む, (～するのを)いやがる
- **have** 動 ①持つ, 持っている, 抱く ②(～が)ある, いる ③食べる, 飲む ④経験する, (病気に)かかる ⑤催す, 開く ⑥(人に)～させる　have to ～しなければならない　don't have to ～する必要はない　have no choice but to ～するしかない　have no idea わからない 助《〈have + 過去分詞〉の形で現在完了の文をつくる》～した, したことがある, ずっと～している　could have done ～だったかもしれない《仮定法》　would have … if ～ もし～だったとしたら…しただろう
- **he** 代 彼は[が]
- **health** 名 健康(状態)
- **hear** 動 聞く, 聞こえる　hear about ～について聞く　hear of ～について聞く
- **heard** 動 hear (聞く)の過去, 過去分詞
- **heart** 名 心臓
- **heavy** 形 重い
- **Heisenberg, Werner** ヴェルナー・ハイゼンベルク《ドイツの理論物理学者, 量子力学に絶大な貢献をした。1901-1976》
- **held** 動 hold (つかむ)の過去, 過去分詞　be held together by ～によって結び付いている
- **help** 動 助ける, 手伝う　help ～ to … ～が…するのを助ける　help in ～に役立つ
- **helper** 名 助手, 助けになるもの

- **her** 代 ①彼女を[に] ②彼女の
- **here** 副 ①ここに[で] ②《- is [are] ~》ここに~がある ③さあ、そら 名 ここ
- **Hermann** 名 ヘルマン《アインシュタインの父、1847-1902》
- **hidden** 動 hide (隠れる)の過去分詞 形 隠れた、秘密の
- **high** 形 高い
- **Hilbert, David** ダフィット・ヒルベルト《ドイツの数学者、1862-1943》
- **him** 代 彼を[に]
- **himself** 代 彼自身
- **Hiroshima** 名 広島《地名》
- **his** 代 ①彼の ②彼のもの
- **history** 名 歴史、経歴
- **hit** 動 ①打つ、なぐる ②ぶつける、ぶつかる ③命中する ④(天災などが)襲う、打撃を与える ⑤hitの過去、過去分詞
- **Hitler, Adolf** アドルフ・ヒトラー《ドイツの政治家、国家社会主義ドイツ労働者党党首として、反ユダヤ主義を掲げる。1939年のポーランド侵攻によって第二次世界大戦を引き起こした。1889-1945》
- **hole** 名 穴
- **home** 名 家、家庭 **at home** 在宅して
- **homeland** 名 母国、祖国、本土
- **honeymoon** 名 新婚旅行
- **hope** 名 希望、期待、見込み 動 望む、(~であるようにと)思う
- **hospital** 名 病院
- **hour** 名 1時間、時間
- **house** 名 ①家、家庭 ②(特定の目的のための)建物、小屋
- **how** 副 ①どうやって、どれくらい、どんなふうに ②なんて(~だろう) ③《関係副詞》~する方法 **how many times** 何回~か
- **Hungary** 名 ハンガリー《国名》
- **hurt** 動 傷つける、痛む、害する

I

- **I** 代 私は[が]
- **idea** 名 考え、意見、アイデア、計画 **have no idea** わからない
- **if** 接 もし~ならば、たとえ~でも、~かどうか **as if** あたかも~のように、まるで~みたいに **ask ~ if** ~かどうか尋ねる **even if** たとえ~でも **If +《主語》+ could** ~できればなあ《仮定法》 **see if** ~かどうかを確かめる **would have … if ~** もし~だったとしたら…しただろう 名 疑問、条件、仮定
- **Ilse** 名 イルゼ《エルザの前夫の子ども》
- **imagination** 名 想像(力)、空想
- **imagine** 動 想像する、心に思い描く
- **immediately** 副 すぐに、~するやいなや
- **important** 形 重要な、大切な、有力な
- **in** 前 ①《場所・位置・所属》~(の中)に[で・の] ②《時》~(の時)に[の・で]、~後(に)、~の間(に) ③《方法・手段》~で ④~を身につけて、~を着て ⑤~に関して、~について ⑥《状態》~の状態で 副 中へ[に]、内へ[に]
- **inside** 前 ~の内部[内側]に
- **institute** 名 協会、研究所
- **insurance** 名 保険
- **intellectual** 形 知的な、知性のある 名 知識人、有識者
- **intelligence** 名 知能
- **intelligent** 形 頭のよい、聡明な
- **interested** 形 興味を持った、関心のある **be interested in** ~に興味[関心]がある
- **interesting** 動 interest (興味を起

こさせる)の現在分詞 形おもしろい, 興味を起こさせる
- **international** 形国際(間)の
- **International Committee on Intellectual Cooperation** 国際知的協力委員会《国際連盟の諮問機関, 1922-1946》
- **into** 前 ①《動作・運動の方向》~の中へ[に] ②《変化》~に[へ]
- **invite** 動 招待する, 招く
- **is** 動 be (~である)の3人称単数現在
- **Isaac Newton** アイザック・ニュートン《イングランドの自然哲学者, 数学者, 1642-1727》
- **island** 名島
- **Israel** 名イスラエル《国名》
- **it** 代 ①それは[が], それを[に] ②《天候・日時・距離・寒暖などを示す》 It is ~ for someone to … (人)が…するのは~だ
- **Italy** 名イタリア《国名》
- **its** 代それの, あれの

J

- **Jakob** 名ヤコブ《アインシュタインの叔父, 1850-?》
- **James Joyce** ジェイムズ・ジョイス《アイルランド出身の小説家, 詩人, 1882-1941》
- **Japan** 名日本《国名》
- **Jew** 名ユダヤ人, ユダヤ教徒
- **job** 名仕事, 職, 雇用 **get a job** 職を得る
- **join** 動 一緒になる, 参加する
- **journal** 名雑誌, 機関誌
- **July** 名7月
- **June** 名6月
- **jungle** 名ジャングル
- **just** 形正しい, もっともな, 当然な 副 ①まさに, ちょうど, (~した)ばかり ②ほんの, 単に, ただ~だけ ③ちょっと

K

- **kaiser** 名《敬称としての》皇帝, カイザー, カイゼル
- **Kaiser Wilhelm Institute** カイザー・ヴィルヘルム協会《ドイツの科学振興のため1911年ヴィルヘルム2世の勅許を得て設立された機関》
- **keep** 動 ①とっておく, 保つ, 続ける ②(~に…)しておく ③飼う, 養う ④経営する ⑤守る **keep up** 続ける, 続く, 維持する, (遅れないで)ついていく, 上げたままにしておく
- **kept** 動 keep (とっておく)の過去, 過去分詞
- **kill** 動殺す
- **kind** 形親切な, 優しい 名種類 **kind of** ある程度, いくらか, ~のような物[人]
- **knew** 動 know (知っている)の過去
- **know** 動 ①知っている, 知る, (~が)わかる, 理解している ②知り合いである **as you know** ご存知のとおり **know of** ~について知っている
- **known** 動 know (知っている)の過去分詞 形知られた **well known** 有名な, 名の通った

L

- **lab** 略研究所, 実験室《laboratoryの略》
- **lady** 名婦人, 夫人, 淑女, 奥さん
- **language** 名言語, 言葉, 国語, ~語, 専門語 **language of nature** 自然が話す言語
- **laser** 名レーザー

- **last** 形《the –》最後の ②この前の、先～ ③最新の 副①最後に ②この前
- **late** 形①遅い、後期の ②最近の ③《the –》故～ 副①遅れて、遅く ②最近まで、以前
- **later** 形もっと遅い、もっと後の 副後で、後ほど
- **law** 名法、法則、法律
- **lazy** 形怠惰な、無精な
- **League of Nations** 国際連盟《第一次大戦の教訓から発足した史上初の国際平和機構、1920–1946》
- **learn** 動学ぶ、習う、教わる、知識[経験]を得る
- **leave** 動①出発する、去る ②残す、置き忘れる ③(～を…の)ままにしておく ④ゆだねる **make someone leave** 退校[職]させる
- **lecture** 名講義、公演 動講義する
- **left** 動leave (出発する)の過去、過去分詞
- **Leo Szilard** レオ・シラード《ハンガリー生まれのアメリカのユダヤ系物理学者、原子爆弾開発に関わった、1898–1964》
- **let's** let us の短縮形
- **letter** 名①手紙 ②文字 ③文学、文筆業
- **level** 名水準
- **library** 名①図書館、図書室
- **life** 名①生命、生物 ②一生、生涯、人生 ③生活、暮らし、世の中
- **light** 名光
- **like** 動好む、好きである **would like to** ～したいと思う 前～に似ている、～のような **look like** ～のように見える、～に似ている 形似ている、～のような 接あたかも～のように 名①好きなもの ②《the [one's] –》同じようなもの[人]
- **limited** 動limit (制限する)の過去、過去分詞 形限られた、限定の

- **liquid** 名液体
- **list** 名名簿、目録、一覧表
- **listen** 動《– to ～》～を聞く、～に耳を傾ける
- **little** 副全然～ない、多少は、やや、《a –》少しはある
- **live** 動住む、暮らす、生きている
- **long** 形①長い、長期の ②《長さ・距離・時間などを示す語句を伴って》～の長さ[距離・時間]の 副長い間、ずっと **no longer** もはや～でない[～しない]
- **look** 動①見る ②(～に)見える、(～の)顔つきをする ③注意する **look back at** ～に視線を戻す、～を振り返って見る **look for** ～を探す **look like** ～のように見える、～に似ている **look out** ①外を見る ②気をつける、注意する **look over** ～越しに見る、～を見渡す
- **looking** 形に見える
- **lost** 動lose (失う)の過去、過去分詞
- **lot** 名たくさん、たいへん、《a – of ～ / -s of ～》たくさんの～
- **love** 名愛、愛情、思いやり **fall in love with** 恋におちる 動愛する、恋する、大好きである
- **luck** 名運、幸運、めぐり合わせ **bad luck** 災難、不運、悪運

M

- **M** 略質量《massの頭文字》
- **made** 動make (作る)の過去、過去分詞 形作った、作られた
- **magnet** 名磁石、引きつけるもの
- **magnetic** 形磁石の、磁気の、引きつける **magnitic fields** 磁界、地場
- **make** 動①作る、得る ②行う、(～に)なる ③(～を…に)する、(～を…)させる **be made to** ～させられる **make a mistake** 間違いをする

- make someone leave 退校[職]させる　make sure 確かめる，確認する
- **man** 名 男性，人，人類
- **Manhattan Project** マンハッタン計画《第二次大戦中，アメリカで進められた原子爆弾開発・製造計画》
- **many** 形 多数の，たくさんの　代 多数(の人・物)
- **manuscript** 名 手書き原稿
- **Marcel Grossmann** マルセル・グロスマン《ハンガリー出身の数学者。アインシュタインに，一般相対性理論の発展に対するリーマン幾何学の必要性を説いた。1878-1936》
- **March** 名 3月
- **Margot** 名 マルゴット《エルザの前夫の子ども》
- **Maric, Mileva** ミレーバ・マリッチ《アインシュタインの最初の妻。1919年に離婚。1875-1948》
- **Marie Winteler** マリー・ヴィンテラー《アインシュタインの最初の恋人》
- **married** 動 marry (結婚する) の過去，過去分詞　形 結婚した，既婚の
- **marry** 動 結婚する
- **mass** 名 ①固まり，(密集した)集まり ②多数，多量 ③質量　動 一団にする，集める，固まる
- **match** 名 適合すること　動 ①〜に匹敵する ②調和する，釣り合う
- **math** 名 数学
- **mathematician** 名 数学者
- **matter** 名 物質
- **Max Planck** マックス・プランク《ドイツの物理学者で量子論の創始者の一人。1858-1947》
- **may** 助 〜かもしれない
- **mean** 動 ①意味する ②(〜のつもりで)言う，意図する
- **measure** 動 ①測る，(〜の)寸法がある ②評価する
- **measurement** 名 ①測定 ②寸法
- **mechanical** 形 機械の，機械的な　mechanical force 機械力
- **meet** 動 ①会う，知り合いになる ②合流する，交わる　meet with 〜に出会う
- **member** 名 一員，メンバー
- **men** 名 man (男性) の複数
- **Mercury** 名 水星《惑星》
- **met** 動 meet (会う) の過去，過去分詞
- **microscope** 名 顕微鏡
- **middle** 名 中間，最中　in the middle of 〜の真ん中[中ほど]に
- **might** 助《mayの過去》〜かもしれない
- **Milan** 名 ミラノ《イタリアの都市》
- **mile** 名 マイル《長さの単位。1,609m》
- **Mileva Maric** ミレーバ・マリッチ《アインシュタインの最初の妻。1919年に離婚。1875-1948》
- **million** 名 ①100万 ②《-s》数百万，多数　形 ①100万の ②多数の
- **mind** 名 心，精神，考え
- **minute** 名 (時間の)分
- **miracle** 名 奇跡(的な出来事)，不思議なこと
- **mistake** 名 誤り，誤解，間違い　make a mistake 間違いをする
- **mixing** 名 (異なる物質の)混合
- **molecule** 名 分子，微粒子
- **moment** 名 ①瞬間，ちょっとの間 ②(特定の)時，時期
- **money** 名 金
- **month** 名 月，1カ月
- **more** 形 ①もっと多くの ②それ以上の　副 もっと，さらに多く，いっそう　代 もっと多くの物[人]　more and more ますます　more than 〜以上　no more もう〜ない

- not ~ any more もう[これ以上]~ない
- **most** 形 ①最も多い ②たいていの,大部分の 代 ①大部分,ほとんど ②最多数,最大限 most of all とりわけ,中でも 副 最も(多く)
- **mother** 名 母,母親
- **motion** 名 運動
- **motor** 名 モーター,発動機
- **mountain** 名 ①山 ②《the ~ M-s》山脈
- **move** 動 ①動く,動かす,移動する move around ~の周りを移動する move away from ~から遠ざかる move on 先に進む move to ~に引っ越す
- **movement** 名 運動
- **movie** 名 映画
- **Mozart** 名 モーツァルト《オーストリアの作曲家。1756–1791》
- **much** 形 (量・程度が)多くの,多量の 副 ①とても,たいへん ②《比較級・最上級を修飾して》ずっと,はるかに too much 過度の
- **Munich** 名 ミュンヘン《ドイツの都市》
- **music** 名 音楽,楽曲
- **musician** 名 音楽家
- **must** 助 ①~しなければならない ②~に違いない
- **mystery** 名 ①神秘,不可思議 ②推理小説,ミステリー

N

- **Nagasaki** 名 長崎《地名》
- **name** 名 ①名前 ②名声 ③《-s》悪口 動 ①名前をつける ②名指しする
- **nation** 名 国,国家,《the ~》国民
- **natural** 形 自然の,天然の
- **nature** 名 ①自然(界) ②天性,性質 ③ありのまま,実物 ④本質

- **Nazi** 名 ナチ,ナチス
- **near** 前 ~の近くに,~のそばに
- **necessary** 形 必要な,必然の
- **need** 動 (~を)必要とする,必要である need to do ~する必要がある 助 ~する必要がある
- **needle** 名 針,針状のもの
- **neither** 形 どちらの~も…でない
- **Nernst, Walter** ヴァルター・ネルンスト《ドイツの科学者,物理学者。1864–1941》
- **nervous** 形 ①神経の ②神経質な,おどおどした
- **Netherlands** 名 オランダ《国名》
- **never** 副 決して[少しも]~ない,一度も[二度と]~ない
- **new** 形 ①新しい,新規の ②新鮮な,できたての
- **New Jersey** ニュージャージー州《アメリカ合衆国の州》
- **New York** ニューヨーク《米国の都市;州》
- **news** 名 報道,ニュース,便り,知らせ
- **Newton, Isaac** アイザック・ニュートン《イングランドの自然哲学者,数学者。1642–1727》
- **next** 形 ①次の,翌~ ②隣の
- **Niels Bohr** ニールス・ボーア《デンマークの理論物理学者。量子力学の確立に貢献,量子力学に反対するアインシュタインと論争を続けた。1885–1962》
- **night** 名 夜,晩 day and night 昼も夜も
- **nine** 名 9(の数字),9人[個] 形 9の,9人[個]の
- **Ninety Mile Beach** 90マイル・ビーチ《オーストラリアの地名》
- **no** 副 ①いいえ,いや ②少しも~ない have no way to ~する道はない no longer もはや~でない[~しない] no more もう~ない there is

WORD LIST

- **no way** ～する見込みはない 形 ～が ない, 少しも～ない, ～どころではない, ～禁止 名 否定, 拒否
- □ **no one** 代 誰も[一人も]～ない
  no one else 他の誰一人として～し ない
- □ **Nobel Prize** ノーベル賞
- □ **normally** 副 普通は, 通常は
- □ **north** 名《the -》北, 北部
- □ **not** 副 ～でない, ～しない not ～ any more もう[これ以上]～ない not ～ at all 少しも[全然]～ない not ～ but … ～ではなくて…
- □ **note** 名 ①メモ, 覚え書き ②注釈 ③注意, 注目 ④手形 動 ①書き留め る ②注意[注目]する
- □ **nothing** 代 何も～ない[しない]
- □ **November** 名 11月
- □ **now** 副 ①今(では), 現在 ②今す ぐに ③では, さて 名 今, 現在 形 今 の, 現在の
- □ **nuclear** 形 核の, 原子力の
  nuclear weapon 核兵器

O

- □ **object** 名 ①物, 事物 ②目的物, 対 象
- □ **observatory** 名 観測所, 気象台, 天文台
- □ **of** 前 ①《所有・所属・部分》～の, ～ に属する ②《性質・特徴・材料》～の, ～製の ③《部分》～のうち ④《分離・ 除去》～から
- □ **off** 副 ①離れて ②はずれて ③止ま って ④休んで get off (～から)降り る 前 ～を離れて, ～をはずれて
- □ **official** 形 公式の, 正式の
- □ **often** 副 しばしば, たびたび
- □ **old** 形 ①年取った, 老いた ②～歳 の ③古い, 昔の 名 昔, 老人
- □ **on** 前 ①《場所・接触》～(の上)に ②《日・時》～に, ～と同時に, ～のす ぐ後で ③《関係・従事》～に関して, ～について, ～して 副 ①身につけて, 上に ②前へ, 続けて
- □ **once** 副 ①一度, 1回 ②かつて 名 一度, 1回 接 いったん～すると
- □ **one** 名 1(の数字), 1人[個] 形 ①1 の, 1人[個]の ②ある ③《the -》 唯一の 代 ①(一般の)人, ある物 ② 一方, 片方 ③～なもの one day (過 去の)ある日, (未来の)いつか one of ～の1つ[人] one side 片側
- □ **oneself** 代 by oneself 一人で, 自 分だけで, 独力で
- □ **only** 形 唯一の 副 ①単に, ～にす ぎない, ただ～だけ ②やっと 接 た だし, だがしかし
- □ **open** 動 開く, 始まる
- □ **or** 接 ①～か…, または ②さもない と ③すなわち, 言い換えると
- □ **orbit** 名 軌道
- □ **other** 形 ①ほかの, 異なった ②(2 つのうち)もう一方の, (3つ以上のう ち)残りの 代 ①ほかの人[物] ②《the -》残りの1つ each other お互いに 副 そうでなく, 別に
- □ **our** 代 私たちの
- □ **out** 副 ①外へ[に], 不在で, 離れ て ②世に出て ③消えて ④すっかり come out of ～から出てくる out of ①～から外へ, ～から抜け出して ② ～の範囲外に, ～から離れて 形 ①外 の, 遠く離れた, ②公表された 前 ～ から外へ[に]
- □ **outside** 名 外部, 外側 形 外部の, 外側の 副 外へ, 外側に
- □ **over** 前 ①～の上の[に], ～を一面 に覆って ②～を越えて, ～以上に, ～ よりまさって ③～の向こう側の[に] ④～の間 副 ①上に, 一面に, ずっと ②終わって, すんで all over ～中で, 全体に亘って be over 終わる
- □ **own** 形 自身の 動 持っている, 所 有する

P

- **Pablo Picasso** パブロ・ピカソ《スペイン出身の美術家。キュビスムの創始者のひとり。1881-1973》
- **pacifist** 名 平和主義者, 無抵抗主義者
- **pain** 名 痛み, 苦悩
- **Palestine** 名 パレスチナ《地名》
- **paper** 名 論文
- **parent** 名《-s》両親
- **part** 名 部分, 割合, 部品
- **particle** 名 粒子, 小さな粒, 微量
- **party** 名 パーティー, 会, 集まり
- **pass** 動 (試験に) 合格する
- **past** 名 過去 (の出来事)
- **patent** 名 特許(権), 特許品 patent clerk 特許審査官 形 特許の
- **Pauline** 名 パウリーネ《アインシュタインの母。1858-1920》
- **Pavia** 名 パヴィーア《イタリアの都市》
- **peace** 名 ①平和, 和解.《the -》治安 ②平穏, 静けさ in peace 平和のうちに, 安心して
- **pen** 名 ペン
- **people** 名 ①(一般に) 人々 ②民衆, 世界の人々, 国民, 民族 ③人間
- **People's Books on Natural Science** 《みんなのための自然科学》《科学入門書。アーロン・ベルンシュタイン著》
- **perfect** 形 完璧な, 完全な
- **person** 名 人
- **PET scan** ポジトロン断層法 (positron emission tomography : PET) スキャン
- **philosopher** 名 哲学者
- **photo** 名 写真
- **photon** 名 光子, 光量子
- **physical** 形 ①物質の, 物理学の, 自然科学の ②身体の, 肉体の
- **physicist** 名 物理学者
- **physics** 名 物理学
- **piano** 名 ピアノ
- **pick** 動 ①(花・果実などを) 摘む, もぐ ②選ぶ, 精選する pick up 拾い上げる
- **picture** 名 写真 take a picture 写真を撮る
- **piece** 名 ①一片, 部分 ②1個, 1本
- **place** 名 ①場所, 建物 ②余地, 空間
- **Planck, Max** マックス・プランク《ドイツの物理学者で量子論の創始者の一人。1858-1947》
- **planet** 名 惑星
- **play** 動 ①遊ぶ, 競技する ②(楽器を) 演奏する, (役を) 演じる play with ~で遊ぶ, ~と一緒に遊ぶ
- **player** 名 演奏者
- **playing card** トランプ (の札)
- **point** 動 (~を) 指す, 向ける
- **poison-gas** 名 毒ガス
- **Polytechnic** 名 技術専門学校
- **poor** 形 ①貧しい, 乏しい, 粗末な, 貧弱な ②劣った, へたな ③不幸な, 哀れな, 気の毒な
- **popular** 形 ①人気のある, 流行の ②一般的な, 一般向きの be popular with ~に人気がある
- **possible** 形 ①可能な ②ありうる, 起こりうる
- **power** 名 力, 能力, 才能, 勢力, 権力
- **powerful** 形 力強い, 実力のある, 影響力のある
- **practice** 動 練習 [訓練] する
- **predict** 動 予測 [予想] する
- **president** 名 大統領
- **Princeton** 名 プリンストン《ニュージャージー州にある都市》
- **Princeton University** プリン

ストン大学《アメリカ合衆国の私立大学》
- **Principe** 名 プリンシペ島《西アフリカのギニア湾に浮かぶ火山島》
- **prize** 名 ①賞, 賞品, 賞金 ②戦利品, 捕獲物 動 高く評価する, 重んじる
- **probably** 副 たぶん, あるいは
- **problem** 名 問題, 難問
- **professor** 名 教授, 師匠
- **project** 名 計画, プロジェクト
- **promise** 動 約束する
- **proof** 名 証拠, 証明
- **property** 名 性質, 属性
- **prove** 動 証明する
- **Prussian Academy** プロイセン科学アカデミー《ベルリンで1700年に設立》
- **publish** 動 出版[発行]する
- **Pugwash Conferences** パグウォッシュ会議《全ての核兵器および戦争の廃絶を訴える科学者による国際会議, 1957–》
- **pull** 動 ①引く, 引っ張る ②引きつける
- **push** 動 ①押す, 押し進む, 押し進める ②進む, 突き出る 名 押し, 突進, 後援
- **put** 動 ①置く, のせる ②入れる, つける ③(ある状態に)する ④putの過去, 過去分詞 **put in** 差し挟む, 応募する **put on** ①~を身につける, 着る ②~を…の上に置く **put out** 外に出す, 出版する, 発行する

Q

- **quantum** 名 量子 **quantum particle** 量子粒子(電子, 原子, イオンなど) **quantum physics** 量子物理学 **quantum theory** 量子(理)論
- **question** 名 質問, 疑問, 問題
- **quit** 動 やめる, 辞職する

R

- **rarely** 副 めったに~しない, まれに, 珍しいほど
- **read** 動 読む, 読書する
- **reader** 名 読者
- **ready** 形 用意[準備]ができた, まさに~しようとする, 今にも~せんばかりの **be ready to** すぐに[いつでも]~できる, ~する構えで
- **real** 形 実際の, 実在する, 本物の
- **really** 副 本当に, 実際に, 確かに
- **reason** 名 理由
- **red** 形 赤い 名 赤, 赤色
- **reject** 動 拒絶する, 断る
- **relativity** 名 関連性, 相対性, 相対論 **general (theory of) relativity** 一般相対性理論 **special (theory of) relativity** 特殊相対性理論
- **remember** 動 思い出す, 覚えている, 忘れないでいる
- **research** 名 調査, 研究
- **respect** 名 尊敬, 尊重 動 尊敬[尊重]する
- **return** 動 帰る, 戻る, 返す **return to** ~に戻る, ~に帰る
- **revolution** 名 革命, 変革
- **rich** 形 富んだ, 金持ちの
- **ride** 動 乗る, 乗って行く, 馬に乗る
- **right** 形 ①正しい ②適切な **all right** 大丈夫で, よろしい, 申し分ない 名 ①正しいこと ②権利
- **roof** 名 屋根(のようなもの)
- **room** 名 ①部屋 ②空間, 余地
- **Roosevelt, Franklin Delano** フランクリン・ルーズベルト《アメリカ合衆国の政治家, 第32代アメリカ大統領, 任期1933–1945》
- **Royal Society** ロンドン王立協会《現存する最も古い科学学会, 1660–》
- **Russell, Bertrand** バートラン

THE ALBERT EINSTEIN STORY

ド・ラッセル《イギリス生まれの論理学者, 数学者, 哲学者。1872-1970》
- **Russia** 名 ロシア《国名》
- **Russian** 名 ロシア(人・語)の 名 ①ロシア人 ②ロシア語

S

- **sad** 形 ①悲しい, 悲しげな ②惨めな, 不運な
- **sadly** 副 悲しそうに, 不幸にも
- **safe** 形 安全な, 危険のない
- **said** 動 say(言う)の過去, 過去分詞
- **same** 形 ①同じ, 同様の ②前述の 代《the -》同一の人[物] 副《the -》同様に
- **sat** 動 sit(座る)の過去, 過去分詞
- **satellite** 名 (人工)衛星
- **saw** 動 see(見る)の過去
- **say** 動 言う, 口に出す
- **saying** 名 言い習わし
- **scan** 名 スキャン, 精査
- **scatter** 動 ①ばらまく, 分散する ②《be -ed》散在する
- **scattering** 名 散乱《波動または粒子線が小物体・分子・原子などにあたって方向を変える事》
- **school** 名 学校
- **science** 名 (自然)科学, 理科, ~学, 学問
- **scientific** 形 科学の, 科学的な
- **scientist** 名 (自然)科学者
- **second** 形 第2の, 2番の
- **secretary** 名 秘書, 書記
- **see** 動 ①見る, 見える, 見物する ②(~と)わかる, 認識する, 経験する ③会う ④考える, 確かめる, 調べる ⑤気をつける see if ~かどうかを確かめる
- **seem** 動 (~に)見える, (~のよう

に)思われる
- **seen** 動 see(見る)の過去分詞
- **sell** 動 売る, 売っている, 売れる
- **sent** 動 send(送る)の過去, 過去分詞
- **serious** 形 ①まじめな, 真剣な ②重大な, 深刻な, (病気などが)重い
- **set** 名 一そろい, セット
- **seven** 名 7(の数字), 7人[個] 形 7の, 7人[個]の
- **share** 動 分配する, 共有する
- **she** 代 彼女は[が]
- **shine** 動 ①光る, 輝く ②光らせる, 磨く
- **shocked** 形 ショックを受けて, 憤慨して
- **shocking** 形 衝撃的な, ショッキングな
- **shoot** 動 (銃を)撃つ
- **short** 形 短い
- **shot** 動 shoot(撃つ)の過去, 過去分詞
- **should** 助 ~すべきである, ~したほうがよい
- **show** 動 ①見せる, 示す, 見える ②明らかにする, 教える ③案内する show someone in [人を]中に案内する, 招き入れる 名 ①表示, 見世物, ショー ②外見, 様子
- **shown** 動 show(見せる)の過去分詞
- **sick** 形 病気の be sick in bed 病気で寝ている
- **side** 名 側, 横, そば, 斜面 one side 片側
- **Sigmund Freud** ジークムント・フロイト《オーストリアの精神分析学者。1856-1939》
- **sign** 動 署名する, サインする
- **since** 接 ①~以来 ②~だから 前 ~以来 副 それ以来
- **sister** 名 姉妹, 姉, 妹

WORD LIST

- sit 動 座る, 腰掛ける
- situation 名 ①場所, 位置 ②状況, 境遇, 立場
- six 名 6(の数字), 6人[個] 形 6の, 6人[個]の
- size 名 大きさ, 寸法, サイズ
- sky 名 空, 天空, 大空
- slow 形 遅い slow child おくての子 副 遅く, ゆっくりと
- slowly 副 遅く, ゆっくり
- small 形 ①小さい, 少ない ②取るに足りない get smaller 小さくなる
- smile 動 微笑する, にっこり笑う
- so 副 ①とても ②同様に, ~もまた ③《先行する句・節の代用》そのように, そう so ~ that … 非常に~なので… 接 ①だから, それで ②では, さて
- socialist 名 社会主義者, 社会党員
- society 名 社会, 世間
- sock 名《-s》ソックス, 靴下
- sold 動 sell(売る)の過去, 過去分詞
- soldier 名 兵士, 兵卒
- Solvay Conferences ソルベー会議《エルネスト・ソルベーとヴァルター・ネルンストが, 1911年に初めて開催した一連の物理学に関する会議》
- some 形 ①いくつかの, 多少の ②ある, 誰か, 何か 副 約, およそ 代 ①いくつか ②ある人[物]たち
- someday 副 いつか, そのうち
- somehow 副 ①どうにかこうにか, ともかく, 何とかして ②どういうわけか
- someone 代 ある人, 誰か
- something 代 ①ある物, 何か ②いくぶん, 多少 something to do 何か~すべきこと
- sometimes 副 時々, 時たま
- son 名 息子, 子弟, ~の子
- soon 副 まもなく, すぐに, すみやかに as soon as ~するとすぐ, ~するや否や
- sorry 形 気の毒に[申し訳なく]思う, 残念な
- sound 動 (~のように)思われる, (~と)聞こえる
- space 名 ①空間, 宇宙 ②すき間, 余地, 場所, 間
- space-time 名 時空《時間と空間を合わせて表現する物理学の用語, または, 時間と空間を同列に扱う概念》
- speak 動 話す, 言う, 演説する speak about ~について話す speak to ~と話す
- special 形 ①特別の, 特殊の, 臨時の ②専門の
- **special (theory of) relativity** 特殊相対性理論
- speech 名 演説, 言語, 語
- speed 名 速力, 速度
- spend 動 ①(金などを)使う, 消費[浪費]する ②(時を)過ごす
- spent 動 spend(使う)の過去, 過去分詞
- spoke 動 speak(話す)の過去
- sport 名 スポーツ
- spring 名 春
- squared 形 平方の, 2乗の
- star 名 星
- start 動 ①出発する, 始まる, 始める ②生じる, 生じさせる start doing ~し始める start to do ~し始める
- station 名 駅
- stay 動 とどまる, 泊まる, 滞在する stay at (場所)に泊まる stay in 家にいる, (場所)に泊まる, 滞在する
- still 副 ①まだ, 今でも ②それでも(なお) 形 静止した, 静かな
- stop 動 ①やめる, やめさせる, 止める, 止まる ②立ち止まる stop doing ~するのをやめる

THE ALBERT EINSTEIN STORY

- **story** 名①物語, 話 ②(建物の)階
- **straight** 形①一直線の, まっすぐな, 直立[垂直]の ②率直な, 整然とした 副①一直線に, まっすぐに, 垂直に ②率直に
- **strange** 形①知らない, 見[聞き]慣れない ②奇妙な, 変わった
- **street** 名街路
- **stretch** 動引き伸ばす, 広がる, 広げる stretch out 広がる
- **strong** 形強い, 堅固な, 強烈な
- **student** 名学生, 生徒
- **study** 動①勉強する, 研究する ②調べる 名①研究 ②書斎
- **success** 名成功, 幸運, 上首尾
- **successful** 形成功した, うまくいった
- **such** 形①そのような, このような ②そんなに, とても, 非常に such a そのような
- **suddenly** 副突然, 急に
- **summer** 名夏
- **sun** 名《the -》太陽, 日
- **support** 動支える, 支持する
- **sure** 形確かな, 確実な make sure 確かめる, 確認する
- **surprised** 動 surprise (驚かす) の過去, 過去分詞 形驚いた
- **Switzerland** 名スイス《国名》
- **Szilard, Leo** レオ・シラード《ハンガリー生まれのアメリカのユダヤ系物理学者, 原子爆弾開発に関わった, 1898-1964》

T

- **T-shirt** 名Tシャツ
- **take** 動①取る, 持つ ②持って[連れて]いく, 捕らえる ③乗る ④(時間・労力を)費やす, 必要とする ⑤(ある動作を)する ⑥飲む ⑦耐える, 受け入れる take ~ to … ~を…に連れて行く take a picture 写真を撮る take a walk 散歩をする take care of ~の世話をする, ~面倒を見る, ~を管理する take in 取り入れる, 取り込む, (作物・金などを)集める take over 引き継ぐ, 支配する, 乗っ取る 名①取得 ②捕獲
- **taken** 動 take (取る) の過去分詞
- **talk** 動話す, 語る, 相談する 名①話, おしゃべり ②演説 《the -》話題
- **tall** 形高い, 背の高い
- **teach** 動教える
- **teacher** 名先生, 教師
- **technique** 名テクニック, 技術, 手法
- **technology** 名テクノロジー, 科学技術
- **telegram** 名電報
- **telescope** 名望遠鏡
- **television** 名テレビ
- **tell** 動①話す, 言う, 語る ②教える, 知らせる, 伝える ③わかる, 見分ける tell ~ to … ~に…するように言う
- **terrible** 形恐ろしい, ひどい, ものすごい, つらい
- **test** 名試験, テスト, 検査 動試みる, 試験する
- **-th** 尾4以上の序数を作る接尾辞
- **than** 接~よりも, ~以上に
- **thank** 名 thanks to ~のおかげで, ~の結果
- **that** 形その, あの 代①それ, あれ, その[あの]人[物] ②《関係代名詞》~である… 接~ということ, ~ので, ~だから so ~ that … 非常に~なので… 副そんなに, それほど
- **the** 冠 ①その, あの ②《形容詞の前で》~な人々 副《- + 比較級, - + 比較級》~すればするほど…
- **their** 代彼(女)らの, それらの
- **them** 代彼(女)らを[に], それら

WORD LIST

を[に]
- **then** 副その時(に・は), それから, 次に 名その時 形その当時の
- **theory** 名理論, 学説
- **there** ①そこに[で・の], そこへ, あそこへ ②《- is [are] ~》~がある[いる] **there is no way** ~する見込みはない 名そこ
- **these** 代これら, これ 形これらの, この
- **they** 代①彼(女)らは[が], それらは[が] ②(一般の)人々は[が]
- **thing** 名①物, 事 ②《-s》事情, 事柄 ③《one's -s》持ち物, 身の回り品 ④人, やつ
- **think** 動思う, 考える **think of** ~のことを考える, ~を思いつく, 考え出す
- **thinker** 名思想家, 考える人
- **thinking** 動think(思う)の現在分詞 名考えること, 思考 形思考力のある, 考える
- **third** 名第3(の人[物]) 形第3の, 3番の
- **this** 形①この, こちらの, これを ②今の, 現在の 代①これ, この人[物] ②今, ここ
- **those** 形それらの, あれらの **in those days** あのころは, 当時は 代それら[あれら]の人[物]
- **though** 接①~にもかかわらず, ~だが ②たとえ~でも **as though** あたかも~のように, まるで~みたいに 副しかし
- **thought** 動think(思う)の過去, 過去分詞 名考え, 意見 **thought experiment** 思考実験
- **thousand** 名①1000(の数字), 1000人[個] ②《-s》何千, 多数 **thousands of** 何千という 形①1000の, 1000人[個]の ②多数の
- **three** 名3(の数字), 3人[個] 形3の, 3人[個]の
- **threw** 動throw(投げる)の過去

- **through** 前~を通して, ~中を[に], ~中
- **throw** 動投げる
- **tie** 動結ぶ, 束縛する
- **time** 名①時, 時間, 歳月 ②時期 ③期間 ④時代 ⑤回, 倍 **all the time** ずっと, いつも, その間ずっと **at a time when** ~という時に **at one time** ある時には, かつては **at the time** そのころ, 当時は **at this time** 現時点では, このとき **how many times** 何回~か **in time** やがて 動時刻を決める, 時間を計る
- **tiny** 形ちっぽけな, とても小さい
- **to** 前①《方向・変化》~へ, ~に, ~の方へ ②《程度・時間》~まで ③《適合・付加・所属》~に ④《- + 動詞の原形》~するために[の], ~する, ~すること **from ~ to …** ~から…まで
- **today** 名今日 副今日(で)は
- **together** 副①一緒に, ともに ②同時に
- **told** 動tell(話す)の過去, 過去分詞
- **too** 副①~も(また) ②あまりに~すぎる, とても~ **too ~ to …** するには~すぎる **too much** 過度の
- **took** 動take(取る)の過去
- **touch** 動①触れる, さわる, ~を触れさせる ②接触する
- **toward** 前①《運動の方向・位置》~の方へ, ~に向かって ②《目的》~のために
- **town** 名町, 都会, 都市
- **toy** 名おもちゃ
- **train** 名列車, 電車
- **translator** 名翻訳者, 通訳者
- **travel** 動①旅行する ②進む, 移動する[させる], 伝わる
- **tree** 名①木, 樹木
- **trip** 名(短い)旅行, 遠征, 遠足, 出張 **go on a trip** 旅行する
- **trouble** 名①困難, 迷惑 ②心配,

107

苦労 ③もめごと
- **true** 形 ①本当の, 本物の, 真の ②誠実な, 確かな **dream come true** 夢がかなった 副 本当に, 心から
- **truth** 名 ①真理, 事実, 本当 ②誠実, 忠実さ
- **try** 動 ①やってみる, 試みる ②努力する, 努める
- **tutor** 名 家庭教師
- **two** 名 2(の数字), 2人[個] 形 2の, 2人[個]の

U

- **Ulm** 名 ウルム《ドイツ連邦共和国の都市》
- **uncle** 名 おじ
- **under** 前 《位置》〜の下[に]
- **understand** 動 理解する, わかる, 〜を聞いて知っている
- **unified field theory** 統一場理論《様々な力を統一しようとする場の理論》
- **United States** 名 アメリカ合衆国《国名》
- **universe** 名 《the – /the U-》宇宙, 全世界
- **university** 名 (総合)大学
- **until** 前 〜まで(ずっと) 接 〜の時まで, 〜するまで
- **up** 副 ①上へ, 上がって, 北へ ②立って, 近づいて ③向上して, 増して 前 ①〜の上(の方) へ, 高い方へ ②(道)に沿って 形 上向きの, 上りの 名 上昇, 向上, 値上がり
- **us** 代 私たちを[に] 略 《US》アメリカ合衆国(=U.S./the United States)
- **use** 動 ①使う, 用いる ②費やす 名 使用, 用途
- **used to** 以前は〜だった, 以前はよく〜したものだった
- **usually** 副 普通, いつも(は)

V

- **very** 副 とても, 非常に, まったく 形 本当の, きわめて, まさしくその **very end** 最後の最後
- **violin** 名 バイオリン

W

- **wait** 動 ①待つ, 《-for 〜》〜を待つ ②延ばす, 延ばせる, 遅らせる ③《-on [upon] 〜》〜に仕える, 給仕をする **wait for** 〜を待つ
- **wake** 動 wake up 起きる, 目を覚ます
- **walk** 動 歩く, 歩かせる, 散歩する **walk around** 歩き回る, ぶらぶら歩く 名 歩くこと, 散歩 **take a walk** 散歩をする
- **Walter Nernst** ヴァルター・ネルンスト《ドイツの科学者, 物理学者。1864-1941》
- **want** 動 ほしい, 望む, 〜したい, 〜してほしい 名 欠乏, 不足
- **war** 名 戦争(状態), 闘争, 不和
- **warp** 動 曲がる, そる, ゆがむ, ゆがませる
- **was** 《be の第1・第3人称単数現在 am, is の過去》〜であった, (〜に)いた[あった]
- **watch** 動 じっと見る, 見物する
- **wave** 名 波, 波動
- **way** 名 ①道, 通り道 ②方向, 距離 ③方法, 手段 ④習慣 **have no way to** 〜する道はない **in this way** このようにして **there is no way** 〜する見込みはない **way to** 〜する方法
- **we** 代 私たちは[が]
- **weak** 形 ①弱い, 力のない, 病弱な ②劣った, へたな, 苦手な
- **weapon** 名 武器, 兵器
- **wear** 動 着る, 着ている, 身につける

WORD LIST

- **weather** 名 天気, 天候, 空模様
- **week** 名 週, 1週間
- **weight** 名 ①重さ, 重力, 体重 ②重荷, 負担 ③重大さ, 勢力
- **weightless** 形 重量のない, 無重力の
- **well** 副 ①うまく, 上手に ②十分に, よく, かなり do well 成績が良い, 成功する very well 結構, よろしい well known 有名な, 名の通った
- **went** 動 go（行く）の過去
- **were** 動《beの2人称単数・複数の過去》〜であった,（〜に）いた［あった］
- **Werner Heisenberg** ヴェルナー・ハイゼンベルク《ドイツの理論物理学者, 量子力学に絶大な貢献をした. 1901-1976》
- **what** 代 ①何が［を・に］《関係代名詞》〜するところのもの［こと］形 ①何の, どんな ②なんと ③〜るだけの 副 いかに, どれほど
- **when** 副 ①いつ《関係副詞》〜するところの, 〜するとその時, 〜するとき 接 〜の時, 〜するとき at a time when 〜という時に 代 いつ
- **where** 副 ①どこに［で］《関係副詞》〜するところの, そしてそこで, 〜するところ where to どこで〜すべきか 接 〜なところに［へ］, 〜するところに［へ］代 ①どこ, どの点 ②〜するところの
- **whether** 接 〜かどうか, 〜かまたは…, 〜であろうとなかろうと
- **which** 形 ①どちらの, どの, どれでも ②どんな〜でも, そしてこの 代 ①どちら, どれ, どの人［物］②《関係代名詞》〜するところの
- **while** 接 ①〜の間（に）, 〜する間（に）②一方, 〜なのに 名 しばらくの間, 一定の時
- **white** 形 白い
- **who** 代 ①誰が［は］, どの人 ②《関係代名詞》〜するところの（人）
- **whole** 形 全体の, すべての, 完全な, 満〜, 丸〜 名《the -》全体, 全部
- **whose** 代 ①誰の ②《関係代名詞》（〜の）…するところの
- **why** 副 ①なぜ, どうして ②《関係副詞》〜するところの（理由）
- **wife** 名 妻, 夫人
- **will** 助 〜だろう, 〜しよう, する（つもりだ）
- **William Wallace Campbell** ウィリアム・キャンベル《アメリカ合衆国の天文学者. 1862-1938》
- **win** 動 勝つ, 獲得する, 達する
- **window** 名 窓, 窓ガラス
- **winner** 名 勝利者, 成功者
- **wish** 動 望む, 願う,（〜であればよいと）思う 名（心からの）願い wish + had + p.p. 〜だったらよかった《仮定法過去》
- **with** 前 ①《同伴・付随・所属》〜と一緒に, 〜を身につけて, 〜とともに ②《様態》〜（の状態）で, 〜して ③《手段・道具》〜で, 〜を使って
- **within** 前 ①〜の中［内］に, 〜の内部で ②〜以内で, 〜を越えないで 副 中［内］へ［に］, 内部に 名 内部
- **without** 前 〜なしで, 〜がなく, 〜しないで
- **woke** 動 wake（目が覚める）の過去
- **woman** 名（成人した）女性, 婦人
- **women** 名 woman（女性）の複数
- **won** 動 win（勝つ）の過去, 過去分詞
- **word** 名 ①語, 単語 ②ひと言 ③《one's -》約束
- **work** 動 ①働く, 勉強する, 取り組む ②機能［作用］する, うまくいく work in 〜の分野で働く, 〜に入り込む work on 〜で働く, 〜に取り組む 名 ①仕事, 勉強 ②職 ③作品 at work 働いて, 仕事中で work of 〜 の作業

109

THE ALBERT EINSTEIN STORY

- □ **worker** 名 仕事をする人, 労働者
- □ **world** 名 《the-》世界, ～界 **in the world** 世界で
- □ **worn** 動 wear (着ている) の過去分詞 形 ①すり切れた, 使い古した ②やつれた, 疲れた
- □ **worried** 動 worry (悩む) の過去, 過去分詞 形 心配そうな, 不安げな
- □ **worry** 動 悩む, 悩ませる, 心配する [させる] **be worried about** (～のことで) 心配している, ～が気になる [かかる] **worry about** ～のことを心配する
- □ **worse** 形 いっそう悪い, より劣った, よりひどい **get worse** 悪化する 副 いっそう悪く
- □ **would** 動 《will の過去》①～するだろう, ～するつもりだ ②～したものだ **would have … if ～** もし～だったとしたら…しただろう **would like to** ～したいと思う
- □ **write** 動 書く, 手紙を書く **write to** ～に手紙を書く
- □ **written** 動 write (書く) の過去分詞 形 文書の, 書かれた
- □ **wrong** 形 ①間違った, (道徳上) 悪い ②調子が悪い, 故障した 副 間違って 名 不正, 悪事
- □ **wrote** 動 write (書く) の過去

Y

- □ **year** 名 ①年, 1年 ②学年, 年度 ③～歳 **for ～ years** ～年間, ～年にわたって
- □ **yellow** 形 黄色の 名 黄色
- □ **yes** 副 はい, そうです 名 肯定の言葉 [返事]
- □ **you** 代 ①あなた (方) は [が], あなた (方) を [に] ②(一般に) 人は **as you know** ご存知のとおり
- □ **young** 形 若い, 幼い, 青年の
- □ **your** 代 あなた (方) の

Z

- □ **Zurich** 名 チューリッヒ《スイスの都市》

E-CAT

English **C**onversational **A**bility **T**est
国際英語会話能力検定

● E-CATとは…
英語が話せるようになるための
テストです。インターネット
ベースで、30分であなたの発
話力をチェックします。

www.ecatexam.com

iTEP

● iTEP®とは…
世界各国の企業、政府機関、アメリカの大学
300校以上が、英語能力判定テストとして採用。
オンラインによる90分のテストで文法、リー
ディング、リスニング、ライティング、スピー
キングの5技能をスコア化。iTEP®は、留学、就
職、海外赴任などに必要な、世界に通用する英
語力を総合的に評価する画期的なテストです。

www.itepexamjapan.com

ラダーシリーズ
The Albert Einstein Story
アインシュタイン・ストーリー

2010年10月10日　第 1 刷発行
2025年 7 月 6 日　第18刷発行

著　者　ジェイク・ロナルドソン

発行者　賀川　洋

発行所　IBCパブリッシング株式会社
　　　　〒162-0804 東京都新宿区中里町29番3号
　　　　菱秀神楽坂ビル
　　　　Tel. 03-3513-4511　Fax. 03-3513-4512
　　　　www.ibcpub.co.jp

© IBC Publishing, Inc. 2010

印刷　株式会社シナノパブリッシングプレス
装丁　伊藤　理恵
組版データ　Sabon Roman + Tw Cen MT Bold

落丁本・乱丁本は、小社宛にお送りください。送料小社負担にてお取り替えいたします。本書の無断複写（コピー）は著作権法上での例外を除き禁じられています。

Printed in Japan
ISBN978-4-7946-0052-3

カバー・本文写真提供：ロイター＝共同

LADDER SERIES